OUT OF THE CAVE

A PHILOSOPHICAL INQUIRY INTO
THE DEAD SEA SCROLLS RESEARCH

Chapter Two
A Hard Look at "Hard Facts": The Archaeology of Qumran 61

Contents

Published with the assistance of
The Aryeh (Leo) Lubin Foundation
in memory of his parents Lilian and Moshe Lubin

The Authority for Research & Development
The Hebrew University of Jerusalem

The book was published in Israel by The Hebrew University Magnes Press,
Jerusalem

Library of Congress Cataloging-in-Publication Data

Ullmann-Margalit, Edna.
  Out of the cave: a philosophical inquiry into the Dead Sea scrolls research
  / Edna Ullmann-Margalit.
  p. cm.
  Includes bibliographical references (p.   ) and index.
  ISBN 0–674–02223–8
  1. Qumran community. 2. Essenes. 3. Excavations (Archaeology) – West
  Bank. 4. Qumran Site (West Bank). 5. Dead Sea scrolls. I. Title.

BM175.Q6U45 2006
296.1'55–dc22   2005033197

Printed in the United States of America
Typesetting: Art Plus, Jerusalem

EDNA ULLMANN-MARGALIT

OUT OF THE CAVE

A PHILOSOPHICAL INQUIRY INTO
THE DEAD SEA SCROLLS RESEARCH

HARVARD UNIVERSITY PRESS
CAMBRIDGE, MASSACHUSETTS
AND LONDON, ENGLAND
2006

of casting a powerful spell, one of a peculiar romantic and social-utopian nature. In the earlier years it was also accompanied by intense expectations that the contents of the scrolls might reveal unmediated contemporary accounts about the birth of Christianity, possibly even about the life of Jesus himself, and in any case bear directly on the sensitive issue of the Jewish roots of Christianity. Could the cryptic epithets the "Teacher of Righteousness," the "Righteous Messiah," the "Wicked Priest," or the "Man of the Lie" possibly refer to New Testament figures such as John the Baptist, Jesus Christ, James the brother of Jesus, or Paul of Tarsus? Could it be that "the historical basis of the Lord's Supper and part at least of the Lord's Prayer and the New Testament teaching of Jesus were attributable to the Qumranites" (as suggested in a *New York Times* report in 1956)?[2]

At the same time there can be no question that public interest in the scrolls was fuelled not only by their contents but by external circumstances as well. The scrolls were from the very outset surrounded by extraordinary circumstances of seemingly endless intrigue, conspiracy, and scandal. These began with the cloak-and-dagger operations involving the acquisition of the first scrolls,[3] and continued with the impact of politics and the effects on

---

2   "Christian Bases Seen in Scrolls," *New York Times*, 5 February 1956, p. 2. See Fitzmyer, 1992, p. 163 for discussion of the context in which this story appeared.

3   Here are excerpts from a fairly dry account (Garcia Martinez, 1996, pp. xxxvi–xxxvii): "Everything begins with the Bedouin of the Ta'amireh tribe. They were the chance discoverers at the start and the passionate prospectors later on, of most of the manuscripts originating from the area of Qumran. In one version of the events it is a shepherd of the tribe, Mohhammed ed-Dib, who in search of a stray goat came across the first of the caves with manuscripts.... In the spring of 1947, seven manuscripts originating from Cave 1 pass into the hands of two 'dealers in antiquities' in Bethlehem.... Four of these seven manuscripts were acquired by Athanasius Yeshue Samuel, the archimandrite of the Syrian–Orthodox monastery in Jerusalem, in the hope of making some profit from their sale. The other three were offered to Professor E. L. Sukenik of the Hebrew University, Jerusalem.... Professor Sukenik understood these manuscripts to be of interest and perhaps to be ancient. He acquired them for the Hebrew University.... In view of the political uncertainty of the country and the problems caused by the setting up of the State of Israel, Mar Athanasius decided to transfer the manuscripts in his possession to the United States with the prospect of selling them."
At this point I switch to the account, by now somewhat of a classic, by Edmund Wilson (1969, pp. 117–118): "[In the summer of 1954] General Yadin – the son of Professor

An artificial cave (Cave 4) in which thousands of fragments, from about 600
scrolls, were found
© The Israel Museum, Jerusalem / by Avraham Hai

The discovery of the scrolls in eleven caves in the Judaean Desert launched
a vast and highly professional field of study. Yet this field has always
commanded unusual popular attention and interest. The contents of the
scrolls succeeded in firing the imagination of the world. A picture emerged
from them of a highly enigmatic religious sect, leading its strict spiritual life
in the wilderness of the arid Judaean Desert. This picture proved capable

Thanks of a different kind go to my mother, Lisa Ullmann, a model classical scholar (whose new translation of Josephus' *The Jewish War*, from Greek to Hebrew, is about to be published): she has been an inexhaustible source of answers to my queries, whether linguistic or historical, none of which to her were ever too large or too small.

It gives me pleasure to gratefully acknowledge the institutional support I had received over the years from the Institute for Advanced Study at Princeton and from the Center for Rationality Research at the Hebrew University of Jerusalem. During the final stages of seeing the manuscript through the press I enjoyed the auspices of the Russell Sage Foundation in New York. I also acknowledge my gratitude to the journal *Social Research* and to its editor, Arien Mack, who published an early version of Chapter One of this book (1998, Volume 65:4).

I cannot imagine my journey into the world of the Dead Sea scrolls without the mentoring of Magen Broshi, the former curator of the Shrine of the Book at the Israel Museum in Jerusalem, where the scrolls are housed. A central protagonist in the scrolls debates and a staunch defender of the dominant theory in the field, Broshi introduced me, directly or indirectly, to everything I know about the scrolls. I am grateful to him in more ways than I can here hope to articulate. Still, perhaps my largest debt to him is that his friendship to me never wavered even when we disagreed. He nobly allowed me the latitude, under his tutelage, to develop my own views that eventually came to diverge from his views at some significant points.

My last, deepest and most special gratefulness is also my first; it belongs to Avishai Margalit, my wise counselor and true partner throughout.

Jerusalem, September 2005

Preface

This book took a long time to gestate. I got progressively drawn into the saga of the Dead Sea scrolls during the 1990s, my initial moderate interest gradually developing into keen fascination. Over the years I have read the literature, attended lectures and conferences, and talked to scholars; I also got to know some of the main protagonists in the Dead Sea Scrolls debates. By 1997, the year marking the 50th anniversary of the discovery of the first scrolls at the site of Qumran, my stance as an outside spectator was giving way to a resolve to become a participant with a contribution of my own to the field of Dead Sea Scrolls research. The central arguments of the field needed to be analyzed: I felt that such an analysis might throw light on this body of research from an angle it had not been much illuminated before. The task I set out for myself, then, was to subject to scrutiny the inner logic of the main theory of Qumran studies as well as of the rival theories, aiming to probe the relentless debates and controversies about these theories that have been raging in the past five decades among the practitioners of the field, scrolls scholars and archaeologists alike.

A number of scrolls researchers were generous toward me with their time, in the early stages of this enterprise. I am grateful to Hanan Eshel, Israel Knoll, Esther Hazon, Daniel Schwartz and David Satran, all of whom had much to teach me. Later on I benefited from, and am thankful for, conversations I had with Albert Baumgarten, Pauline Donceel-Voûte, Norman Golb, Yizhar Hirschfeld, Jodi Magness, and Yaacob Sussmann. I wish also to thank non-Qumranologists Hilary Putnam, Jerry Cohen and Michael Walzer, whose encouragement was given when it was most needed. Additional gratitude I owe to Harry Frankfurt, Menachem Fisch, Daniel Schwartz and Cass Sunstein, who read early chapter versions and gave me valuable comments, and most specially to Jonathan Malino, who much improved my final manuscript in both form and substance.

fell to Qimron, who was deeply hurt when his work was published in full in the U.S. without even a footnote mentioning his name.

The scrolls were found in what was Jordanian territory and were opened up to an international research team. When the Rockefeller Museum passed into Israeli control, the Antiquities Authority continued to allow the international research team access to the scrolls. Qimron joined the team in the 1980s. Those researchers who were denied access to the team claimed that it was a "monopoly" and demanded that it be opened up to all scientists. The objective of the 1991 book, which plagiarized Qimron's work, was protest against this monopoly.

A similar story appeared that same day in the *New York Times*, the *International Herald Tribune*, and elsewhere. It was by no means the first time that an item connected with the Dead Sea scrolls made front-page news.

This particular story tells of a courtroom battle. It relates to the vexing and rather limited issue of copyright protection of the scholarly reconstruction of ancient texts.[1] But even this brief journalistic report of a narrow legal case contains many of the elements that account for the drama that has surrounded the Dead Sea Scrolls for more than fifty years. It mentions a mysterious sect in the Judaean Desert whose members led a communal life under strict rules of conduct. It talks about the incredible jigsaw-puzzle task of piecing together numerous torn fragments of one particular scroll and of the supreme scholarly competence, both linguistic and halakhic, required for deciphering them. It alludes, ever so cryptically ("When the Rockefeller Museum passed into Israeli control") to the 1967 June war and to the effect geo-politics always had on the fate of the scrolls research. And it refers to the passions that ran high regarding the so-called monopoly held over the scrolls by the international research team entrusted with their publication.

---

1   As it happens, this case spurred a controversy among legal scholars: see Nimmer, 2001, and Elkin-Koren, 2001.

Introduction

On Thursday, 31 August 2000, a headline across the front page of the Israeli daily newspaper *Ha'aretz* declared: "Scholar Wins Battle over Dead Sea Scrolls." The article went on to inform the readers:

> A Ben-Gurion University professor yesterday won his eight-year long fight to receive recognition for deciphering sections of the Dead Sea Scrolls, which were published in the U.S. without him receiving any credit.
>
> In 1992 Professor Elisha Qimron petitioned the Jerusalem District Court to stop the distribution of the book *A Facsimile Edition of the Dead Sea Scrolls*, published in the U.S., which contained excerpts from the scroll called *Miqsat Ma'ase ha-Torah* that Qimron had deciphered, but for which he had not receive any credit. Judge Dalia Dorner found in Qimron's favor. The defendants, publisher Hershel Shanks and editors Dr. James Robinson and Dr. Robert Eisenman, appealed to the Supreme Court. The appeal took seven years, ending yesterday in victory for Qimron.
>
> Qimron spent 11 years deciphering 70 torn fragments of the scroll until he managed to put together 121 lines of text, and even gave the scroll its name. The scroll was discovered in the 1950s in a cave near Qumran along with 15,000 fragments of other scrolls, written in a language that pre-dates that used in the Mishnah. The scroll contains a set of regulations ordering the life of the members of the "Yahad," a group within the Judaean Desert sect, who chose to live communally and whose members accepted strict rules of conduct.
>
> Harvard University's John Strugnell was the researcher who pieced the scroll together, but he lacked the necessary background in language and *halakhah* to be able to decipher it. That responsibility

A central theory has dominated Dead Sea Scrolls research since its inception. This theory relates to the enigmatic origins of the scrolls, and it is known as the *Qumran–Essene hypothesis*. It asserts that the scrolls found in the caves belonged to the sect of the Essenes whose center, or "motherhouse," was at the nearby site of Khirbet Qumran. This hypothesis was bolstered by a powerful combination of factors not often encountered in the history of science: textual evidence and an enigmatic archaeological site that seemed to strongly support it, charismatic scholars who propagated it, and a widespread eagerness to believe it. My main concern is with this hypothesis and with the vicissitudes of its career. I am interested in its formulation, its inner logic, the attempts to refute it, and the ways it survives these attempts.

My interest in the hypothesis as a whole leads me to break it up into its constituent elements: why Essenes, why Qumran, why a sect? The three chapters that follow take up each of these concerns in turn. The first deals with the Essene connection, the second with the archaeology of Qumran, and the third with the sectarian nature of the scrolls community, whether Essene or not. Each of the three concerns is an arena in which contesting theories do battle.

Much of the scrolls-related and archaeology-related material is interesting in and of itself. Still, an important part of the intrinsic interest is generated from the interplay between the textual interpretation of the scrolls, on the one hand, and the interpretation of the archaeological site, on the other. In what follows, then, while the scrolls loom large as do the main archaeological features of the Qumran compound, my focus is mostly on the way the interpretations of these two sets of materials feed upon and interact with each other.

Qumran research is unusual in that it offers a large number of choice examples of issues that philosophers of science are often hard put to exemplify. These include questions about hard and tangible facts as opposed to soft or "fungible" facts, and about how facts are framed. Also, questions about the impact of ideology on research (for example, whether researchers want the scrolls to be interpreted and recognized as an internal Jewish affair or as providing a link to Christianity), and about the notion of interpretive circles (for example, what happens when texts are used to interpret material

the scrolls research of two Arab–Israeli wars (1948 and 1967). Allegations that the Vatican was repressing sensitive scroll materials followed, and then came high-pitched international crises involving charges of monopoly, delay in publication, and breach of copyright.

All citizens in the republic of letters of Western civilization are justified in feeling they have a stake in the unfolding story of research on the Dead Sea scrolls and its findings. All the more so a person like myself, whose native tongue is the language of the scrolls and who resides little more than a stone's throw from the Shrine of the Book in Jerusalem, where the scrolls are on permanent display, and a thirty-minute drive from the site of Qumran. Like so many others, I found myself irresistibly drawn to the story of the scrolls, to its puzzles and mysteries. The more immersed I became and the more fascinating I found its details, the deeper my respect grew for the immense scholarship manifested in this research. At the same time, I became convinced of the need to resist the notion that the story of the scrolls ultimately belongs to Qumranologists alone.

This book is the outcome of a personal journey into the territories of Dead Sea Scrolls research. My professional vehicle is philosophy, and my tools are the conceptual tools of an analytical philosopher trained in the philosophy of science. The result is intended for the general interested audience, not solely the Qumran specialists, or the specialists in philosophy of science.

Sukenik – visited the United States.... He wrote the Metropolitan a letter, to which he received no reply, and he concluded that it would not be possible for the Syrians, under the circumstances, to sell the scrolls openly to Israel.... The general's attention, however, was drawn to an ad in the *Wall Street Journal* that appeared during the first three days of June under the heading 'Miscellaneous for sale':

The Four Dead Sea Scrolls
Biblical manuscripts dating back to at least 200 BC
are for sale. This would be an ideal gift to an educational
or religious institution by an individual or group.

Yadin, without letting his name appear, applied to purchase the scrolls, employing as intermediary a lawyer not associated with Israeli business, who negotiated the sale through a New York bank....The price was $250,000....The whole matter was kept a secret until the scrolls had been transported to Israel."

remains for the specialized archaeologist to pronounce judgment about whether the clay jars in which the scrolls were found are unique to Qumran, or whether the similar jars found in Jericho are sufficiently alike so as to undermine the Qumran jars' claim to uniqueness. But it is in order for me to reflect on the possible implications of an answer either way, as well as to raise questions about the role of the uniqueness of archaeological finds in the formation of theories by the archaeologists.

Research of this kind raises the question of who is an expert on the experts. Socrates, famed for claiming to know only that he did not know, nevertheless considered himself capable of sifting the experts from the non-experts with regard to any topic. My experience with Dead Sea Scrolls scholars alerts me to the extent to which their opinion of anyone who is not of their "school" is poor, often quite beyond the normal standards of academic mean-spiritedness. It is striking that the "outsider," the one who holds a rival theory, is for the Qumranologists almost never simply wrong or mistaken: there are rarely disagreements as far as they are concerned, but rather profound misunderstandings, or more often lack of credentials and hence lack of proper standing. The outsider forever misunderstands, is not in the profession, or is a charlatan.

True, the threshold of scholarly competence required for doing worthy research in Qumranology, whether in dealing with the texts of the scrolls or with the archaeology of the site, is high. At the same time it is also true that, these high standards notwithstanding, Qumranology is highly popular. Many are attracted to the scrolls, like moths to the burning lamp, and too many of them lack the required competence for contributing anything of real value to this research. These circumstances understandably serve to strengthen the defensive walls of suspicion surrounding the discipline in general, and the mainstream view in particular. And these walls of suspicion, in turn, are responsible for the eerie feeling one sometimes gets, that in dealing with the Dead Sea scrolls one is facing a sectarian phenomenon not only as regards the authors of the scrolls, but as regards their researchers as well.

Crackpots often display a syndrome that may be termed a *Galileo complex*. The Galileo complex characterizes "outsiders" who view

archaeological finds while the texts are being simultaneously interpreted by these very finds).

Not only scholars are attracted to the scrolls. Over the years many crackpots, whether religious or scientific, have offered theories and solutions to what were generally perceived as the mysteries of the scrolls, their provenance, and their message. In response, walls of suspicion were gradually raised around the scholarly disciplines relating to scrolls research, separating "insiders" from "outsiders." Anyone without specialized training in archaeology, papyrology, paleography, biblical or early-Christian or halakhic studies, ancient Near Eastern history, or any other discipline that is intrinsic to the bona fide scrolls-related research, is likely to be dismissed as belonging to the usual suspects: pseudo-scholars, frauds, or charlatans. Since I myself am not a scrolls scholar, I too may be suspect. I need therefore to say something about how I see my standing in this matter.

To me the important distinction here is between the ground-level phenomena and upper-level reflection upon them – or, as this is customarily referred to, between first-order and second-order scholarship. My subject matter is not the scrolls but the study of the scrolls; I engage in research about scrolls research and delve into its inner logic.

Not much insight or enlightenment can be expected from exercises in formal logic. But some insight and enlightenment can be expected from distinguishing between substantive research into a subject matter and the second-order level of reflection about it. My concern, then, embraces topics that are generally dealt with by philosophers of science, topics that have to do with the assessment of the relationship between evidence and hypotheses, with questions relating to the confirmation and refutation of hypotheses, with evaluating the validity of arguments (whether deductive or inductive–probabilistic), and more.

The distinction between first- and second-order research is itself of course not a clean or clear-cut distinction. When dealing with a discipline as specific, complex, and rich as Dead Sea Scrolls research, no interesting observations on the second-order level can be had unless one immerses oneself quite deeply into the details of the substantive first-order research itself, where in any case much of the fascination with the scrolls inheres. Still, it is well to try to keep the distinction in mind. So, for example, it

themselves as persecuted, or censored, or ignored by orthodoxy (or "mainstream" or "hegemonic doctrine"); it also includes the conviction that ultimately they will prove to possess the big and final truth. This syndrome is dangerous. The more outlandish one's "theory," the more one becomes a self-styled victim, even a martyr, and the more likely one then becomes to attract media attention. There is no doubt that in a scholarly field that is so popular and is so often in the news anyway, it is the unconventional views that tend to occupy center stage. This can sometimes be damaging to scholarly integrity and to the reputation of the field. On the whole, in Qumran studies, as elsewhere, crackpots are crackpots and one may feel reasonably confident that the prospects that there is a Galileo among them are quite negligible.

The task I set for myself inherently requires me to canvass the range of rival, alternative theories about the writings (Who wrote the scrolls?) and about the ruins (What was the site of Qumran?). It is the richness – and the juiciness – of the range that makes this enterprise attractive from the point of view of the philosophy of science, where methodological talk of "alternative theories" often remains speculative and barren for lack of good examples. However, the very mention of some of the alternative theories in Qumran study and the very citation of some of their authors' names is, to many within the mainstream, like the waving of a red cloth in front of a bull. Since to the mainstream scholars the alternatives are by and large crackpot theories, the mere fact that I discuss these theories is liable to taint me by association. I stand the danger, in other words, that the respected scholars in the field will see me as unable to distinguish between real experts and sham experts; from there it is but a very short step to finding me suspect too.

It should by now be clear that I do not discuss the range of alternative theories in order to suggest that they are all equally plausible, nor even that they are plausible at all. The fact that a theory is mentioned and discussed here should not be interpreted as conferring upon it a stamp of approval, whether scholarly or probabilistic or whatever. It should be taken only to indicate that the theory is to be found in the marketplace of ideas. It usually also indicates that the theory is reputably published, and that its author participates in international academic conferences. True, some if not most of the unconventional Dead Sea Scrolls theories are subscribed to by their author alone. Still, as long as they are not altogether initially outlandish,[4] I have not ruled them out for illustrating the points I am concerned to make.

At an early stage in my work on this book I overheard the following statement made to a group of youngsters visiting the Shrine of the Book at the Israel Museum: "Twelve incompatible theories have been proposed as to who wrote the Dead Sea scrolls. Obviously, eleven of them have to be wrong."[5] A presentation of the rudiments of the mainstream, Qumran–Essene theory then followed. On hearing this statement my knee-jerk reaction was to interject, "*at least* eleven." Surely if anything is at all obvious, a priori, it is that all twelve theories may be wrong and that the one true theory still awaits discovery.

I have since come to change my mind, or my perspective, somewhat, on this matter. On the one hand, given the quality of scholarship embedded in the body of research on the Dead Sea scrolls, I am now inclined to believe that, while in principle possible, it is highly unlikely that "the true theory" has so far entirely eluded the scholars. Yet, on the other hand, I have come to realize that it is quite mistaken to think of all the rival theories as discrete, non-interacting monads, so to speak. The tendency on the part of the mainstream scrolls scholars to dismiss as illegitimate any alternative theory blinds them to the fact that their own theory has itself undergone changes over the years. The rival theories, whether eleven, or seven, or seventeen, have not failed to leave their marks on the dominant Qumran–Essene theory, however much this may be denied by some of the mainstream scholars. In this these scholars exemplify a phenomenon referred to as

---

4   As an example consider the case of Barbara Thiering. She claims that the scrolls are the product of rivalry between the supporters of John the Baptist, identified with the scrolls' "Teacher of Righteousness," and Jesus, identified with the "Man of the Lie." For my purposes this theory must be considered altogether initially outlandish, given the scientifically definitive dating (based mostly on paleographical and on radiocarbon techniques) of the scrolls to a period well before the birth of Christianity (Thiering, 1992). Thiering's theory, by the way, is a good example of a fringe theory that is popular with the media.

5   On this see Broshi and Eshel, 2004.

phonetic fanaticism: the stubborn belief that if you fanatically adhere to the same phonetic formula you may go on refusing to acknowledge the changes its meaning has undergone. As I try to show (in Chapter One), the Qumran–Essene theory has found ingenious ways of co-opting some of its challengers so that, subtly adapted and re-described, it endures as the reigning consensus in Qumran studies. And this, as far as I can judge, is as it should be.

This study relates, as I said, to three clusters of questions concerning the Dead Sea scrolls. They deal, in turn, with the Essene connection, with the nature of the site of Qumran, and with the issue of sectarianism. The answers I seek relate to facts and circumstances that are more than two thousand years old. They are buried in torn and corrupt fragments of texts and in scant material artifacts. All that scholars can do in their attempt to get to the truth is to interpret this material, soft facts as well as hard facts, as best they can. And in so doing they are inevitably influenced by their personal hopes and beliefs, as well as by their political, social, religious, and cultural settings. So in the end, the deep-level theme of this inquiry is interpretation and interpretive circles.

The bulk of Chapter One has to do with a grand interpretive circle. Introduced as the "Linkage Argument," this circle is shown to connect the Essenes, the scrolls and the site of Qumran. More specifically it connects, in the first place, between two different sets of textual materials: the scrolls on the one hand, and historical writings of three first-century Greek and Latin authors on the other. Forming a kind of embedded smaller circle within the larger one, information about the Essenes from the first-century historical texts serves as guide to interpreting the scrolls, at the same time as the scrolls are used as a means of understanding the first-century historians. Both sets of textual materials are then connected, in the larger circle, with the archaeological materials from the excavation of the site of Qumran.

With the Linkage Argument underlying the dominant Qumran–Essene hypothesis, questions arise about the nature of the circularity involved and how vicious or benign it might be. While small diameter circles are an obvious embarrassment to scholars because of their dubious explanatory power, the case may be different with the Linkage Argument. Large in diameter, rich and "thick" as it is shown to be, the circle forming the Linkage Argument lays serious claim to scholarly legitimacy. The case is made that this interpretive circle might be stronger than each of its constituent links.

Another fundamental issue of circularity comes up in Chapter Two, in the context of discussing instances in which scholars vary greatly in their initial ("prior") assessment of how probable a given hypothesis is. The theory interpreting the site of Qumran as an Essene monastery is an example of such a hypothesis. According to the Bayesian approach to probabilistic reasoning, the weight of accumulative evidence ought to assure that, in the long run, initially divergent degrees of scholars' belief in the hypothesis will eventually converge – provided that the scholars are rational and agree on the evidence. In the case of the Qumran-qua-monastery hypothesis, however, such convergence of belief does not occur.

In an attempt to account for this non-convergence I offer a conjecture. It is that widely different assignments of prior probability to a theory, inasmuch as they do not attest to the irrationality of some of the scholars involved, they are indicative of deep disagreements among these scholars about the evidence. That is, people who start out with very different assessments about how probable a given theory is will generally be unable to agree about the description and interpretation of almost any piece of evidence that is adduced in support of the theory. Their very description (or "framing") of the evidence will depend on their degree of belief in the theory being tested. For example, the degree to which one will acquiesce with the description of the animal bones found in Qumran as "bone deposits" or "bone burials" – rather than, say, as mere bone leftovers – depends on the degree to which one subscribes to the theory that the occupants of Qumran were a religious sect.

And so we get yet another underlying interpretive circle: one's description of the evidence that is adduced in support of a given theory will depend upon the prior probability one assigns to this very theory, which is in turn influenced by one's background beliefs and general outlook. I believe that this conjecture applies, beyond Qumranology, to the human sciences in general. In the final analysis the deep divisions in the human sciences do not reflect disagreements about bare facts but rather disagreements about meaning and interpretation.

My aim in this chapter is to examine the formation of this theory, its inner logic and its remarkable resilience. Tracing the logic of the theory will bring to light an intriguing interplay between the textual interpretations of the scrolls, on the one hand, and the interpretation of material archaeological finds, on the other. This interplay will be shown to form a thick "circle of interpretation" where texts are used to interpret – and in turn are being interpreted by – material finds. The resilience displayed by the theory in face of numerous attempts to refute it is shown to derive, in the first place, from the strength of the interpretive circle itself. It is also shown to be due to the elasticity of the theory: the peculiar ability of the theory to co-opt some of the hypotheses meant to contest it as well as to adapt itself to them.

General familiarity with the story of the scrolls will be helpful for what follows. I shall start therefore by laying out the background facts.

SETTING THE STAGE

Discovery

In the spring of 1947 a few Bedouin shepherds made the first discovery of scrolled manuscripts in a cave in the Judaean Desert, by the site of Qumran on the north–western shore of the Dead Sea. This find soon led to a "scroll rush"[1] by both Bedouin and archaeologists. By the time it ended in 1956, ten more caves containing manuscripts were found. Altogether they yielded a number of full-length scrolls (up to 22–23 feet long) and tens of thousands of fragments. The manuscripts are mostly on thin parchment, written in ink on the hairy side, and miraculously preserved by the dry desert air but still varying greatly in their degree of preservation as well as in their length. They belong to about 900 manuscripts comprising 300 different compositions, many represented by more than one copy. Of these texts roughly two hundred are biblical, predating the earliest previously known surviving Hebrew biblical texts by at least one thousand years. The other texts are non-biblical, most of them in Hebrew and the rest in

---

1　　The expression is from Stendahl, 1992, p. 1.

CHAPTER ONE

Writings and Ruins:
The Essene Connection

OVERVIEW

Qumran Studies is a field of research which has arisen as a result of the discovery of important scrolls at the site of Qumran by the Dead Sea, more than fifty years ago. Bringing together the study of ancient texts, on the one hand, and archaeological research on the other, this field was born in drama and ever since it remains suffused with controversy. To this day it commands an unusual degree of popular attention and interest.

A scientific field of research is itself sometimes the object of study by philosophers. This book takes up Qumran Studies as its object, focusing mostly on its central theory which relates to the enigmatic origins of the scrolls. This theory, dominant in the field since its inception, is known as the Qumran–Essene hypothesis. It asserts that the scrolls found in the caves belonged to the sect of the Essenes and that the Essene center, or "motherhouse," was at the nearby site of Khirbet (=ruins of) Qumran. The Essenes are believed to have lived at the site of Qumran for more than 150 years (roughly, from 135–100 BCE to 68 CE), where they led a strict communal life distinguished as celibate and highly ritualized. According to the theory it was at Qumran that the Essenes wrote, and copied, the scrolls.

---

*   An early version of this chapter first appeared in *Social Research* 65:4 (1998), pp. 839–870.

Aramaic and Greek. The majority of the texts from this latter category were previously unknown.

Prominent among the non-biblical scrolls are those that were the first to be discovered in Cave 1 and which, as it happens, are the longest and most intact. From their contents there emerges a picture of a reclusive and radical community, which consequently was immediately conjectured to be sectarian in nature. For example, the *Manual of Discipline*, later referred to as the *Rule of the Community*, contains detailed descriptions of the initiation rite into the Covenant of the community, of its penal code, and of its rules for communal life and for the assembly of members. It also contains the theological tenets of the community, such as the doctrine of predestination and the doctrine of the two spirits – the spirit of truth and the spirit of iniquity – which God has created to govern human life.[2]

The *War Scroll* contains instructions for an eschatological war. This will be a forty-year war that the community, referred to as "the Sons of Light," will wage at the end of time against its enemies, "the Sons of Darkness." The text describes the military equipment, army formations, and plans for battle, as well as the prayers and battle-liturgy exhortations that are to be pronounced by the high priest. The scroll of scriptural commentary known as *Pesher Habakkuk*, also found in Cave 1, exemplifies a literary genre that came to light for the first time with the discovery of the Dead Sea scrolls. As a literary form, the *Pesher*, which means interpretation, proceeds by quoting verse by verse directly from the Hebrew Bible, usually from one of the minor prophets, and then commenting on it. The comments relate the words of the prophet (Habakkuk, in this case) to the historical reality

---

2   The well known formulation of these doctrines occurs in the *Rule of the Community* III.13–IV. 26. Their essence is expressed thus: "Before ever they existed He established their whole design, and when, as ordained for them, they come into being, it is in accord with His glorious design that they accomplish their task without change.... All the children of righteousness are ruled by the Prince of Light and walk in the ways of light, but all the children of injustice are ruled by the Angel of Darkness and walk in the ways of darkness" (Vermes, 1998). David Flusser discusses the doctrine of predestination and the tensions between it and the doctrine of the two spirits, or two ways (Flusser, 1997, p. 95). Of the predestination doctrine he asserts that "it was the most important novelty of the Qumran sect, when it crystallized from the wider apocalyptic movement into the sect of the Essenes."

or to theological tenets of the Qumran community. "It is thus a very definite sectarian composition, which would not be current even in Jewish circles outside of this community. The commentary is composed with the conviction that what the prophet of old wrote had pertinence not only to his own times, but also to the life of this community" (Fitzmyer, 1992, p. 33).[3]

Reception and Expectations

It is hard to overstate the excitement generated by the discovery of the scrolls. It became standard to call it the most important (or "the most sensational": Frank, 1992, p. 3)[4] archaeological find of the twentieth century. The description of the discovery was always dramatic: "The discovery of those momentous documents sent shock waves throughout the world of biblical and historical scholarship.... It was as though a miraculous tele-time-scope had suddenly zoomed through a two-thousand-year screen to provide a dramatic close-up of the scenes in the Holy Land during the final centuries of Jewish independence and the birth of Christianity" (Yadin, 1985, p. 8).

The expectations created by the discovery were equally great. The documents held out the unique promise of shedding direct light on a period of particular interest and importance in the history of the West: the two-century period leading up to the destruction of Jerusalem and its Temple by the Romans in 70 CE. It is thus the formative period in the development of the two major religious movements of the Western world. Not only was Christianity born in this period but so was normative (or rabbinic) Judaism. Still, amid the excitement and expectations generated by the discovery of the scrolls, pressing questions had to be addressed: were these manuscripts authentic, when were they written, who wrote them, and what did they tell us?

Scholarship

The decade following the discovery of the seven major scrolls in the first cave was one of intense scholarly activity. While scholars set out to work on the documents, a parallel effort was begun by archaeologists. In

---

3   See also pp. 58–60 below.
4   See also Sussmann, 1994, pp. 179–200 (at least three times).

1951, pottery was found in the site of Khirbet Qumran which struck the excavators as significantly similar to the pottery unearthed in nearby Cave 1. As a result, between 1951 and 1956 a complete excavation of the Qumran ruins was undertaken, under the direction of Roland de Vaux, director of the École Biblique et Archéologique in (Jordanian) Jerusalem. De Vaux himself acknowledged that it was "justifiable" that the enormous interest aroused by the Dead Sea discoveries "should be concentrated above all on the texts." But, he added, "the archaeologist can make a contribution to the understanding of the texts by indicating the nature of the setting in which they were discovered and so perhaps making it possible to reconstruct the character of the human group from which they emerged" (de Vaux, 1973, p. viii).

This statement establishes a close link between the study and interpretation of the writings and the study and interpretation of the ruins. At the same time, the statement is rife with presuppositions: not only are the site of Qumran, the caves, and the scrolls closely linked, but the scrolls are taken to have emerged from the group of people who occupied the site. These presuppositions reflect – at the same time as they helped shape – the view, or theory, which very soon established itself as dominant among Dead Sea Scrolls researchers.

By the end of the first decade (summed up, for example, in Milik 1959) the initial questions assumed sharper contours. As many of the fragments were being pieced together and interpreted, scholars began addressing diverse issues of an increasingly complex nature. The problem of dating the scrolls broke up into several distinct questions (Yadin, 1992a, p. 161; Schiffman, 1994, p. 31): When and in which order were the texts of the scrolls composed? When were the scrolls that were found actually copied? When were they gathered together and deposited in the caves? Further questions concerned the identity of the group (or groups) who composed the texts and the identities of its leaders and opponents. Yet other questions concerned:

• the differences between the versions of the biblical scrolls and the earliest so-called *masoretic* (or traditional) texts of the Bible – and the implications of these differences for the evolution of the canonical Hebrew Bible;

- the connections, if any, between the scrolls and the New Testament, or, more generally, the connections, if any, between the scroll community and early Christianity;
- the light cast by the scrolls on the historical events of the Second Temple period;
- the nature of the *halakhah* (the body of Jewish ritual and law) governing the life of the scrolls community;
- the significance of the archaeological finds at the site of Qumran and their relationship to the owners of the scrolls.

As can readily be seen, there is much disciplinary diversity among these issues. The research generated by the discovery of the Dead Sea scrolls requires, among others, historians of the Second Temple period in Palestine, Bible scholars, scholars of the New Testament and early Christianity, students and historians of *halakhah*, paleographers, linguists and philologists – and archaeologists. In addition, experts in such specialized areas as heresiology and the sociology of religious sects, early Gnosis, the Apocrypha and Pseudepigrapha, and Jewish liturgy must be consulted. All of this interdisciplinary research is subsumed under the title of the Dead Sea Scrolls Studies (DSS), or Qumran Studies (or, as Krister Stendahl is fond of referring to it, "the field of Qumraniana"; Stendahl, 1992, p. x).

The field of Qumran Studies, then, is a highly diverse field of research and activity. It is known to be a field abounding with scholarly debate and controversy and infused with energy. Scores of books and hundreds of scholarly papers are published every year, international seminars and conferences are conducted amid much commotion, and in recent years Qumran-related websites are gushing with activity. Moreover, interest in this field is not confined to its practitioners. News about fresh discoveries concerning the scrolls or the latest controversies that surround them often appear in major newspapers, sometimes making front-page news.[5]

---

5   On 22 September 1991, a three-column headline at the top of the front page of the Sunday *New York Times* declared: "Monopoly over Dead Sea Scrolls is Ended." Around that time, in the summer and fall of 1991, articles and letters appeared in the *Times* of London, the *New York Times*, the *Chicago Tribune*, the *Los Angeles Times*, *Liberation*, *Le Figaro*, *Ha'aretz*, and more. (See Golb, 1995, esp. notes to chapters 8

Popular Interest

Why is this so? Why does news about Qumran research command intense curiosity internationally? How is it that such reports easily transcend the boundaries of interest normally given to academic or scientific news and succeed in invading the popular press and igniting popular imagination? I believe that this is an important question and that meaningful answers to it may yield dividends in terms of providing important insights into central aspects of Qumran research itself. I suggest that in trying to understand this phenomenon we have to look in two separate directions. First, there are internal explanations. These have to do with the actual contents of Dead Sea Scrolls research – that is, if you will, with the curricular record of the field. The other direction involves external explanations. These have to do not with what the research is about but rather with circumstances surrounding it, or with the extra-curricular record of the field.

Explanations of the first sort draw first and foremost on the fact, already mentioned, that from the start there were intense expectations that the contents of the scrolls might bear directly on the inception of Christianity, possibly even on the persons of John the Baptist and Jesus themselves. Related to this were expectations that material contained in the scrolls might touch upon and illuminate the sensitive issue of the Jewish roots of Christianity. In addition to this, however, there is also the undeniable allure of the very connection of the scrolls with the Essenes. The appeal to the reading public of everything to do with the esoteric sect of the Essenes was already appreciated by the first-century author Josephus, and it seems capable of casting a powerful romantic spell on a wide range of audiences to this day.

---

and 10.) These are salient examples, but there are many more. While this book was being prepared for publication, on July 30, 2004 the Hebrew daily *Ha'aretz* carried the following headline as its top front-page news: "Archaeologists Claim Essenes Never Wrote Dead Sea Scrolls." The body of the article informs *Ha'aretz*'s readers that, "based on findings soon to be published, Israeli archaeologists now argue that Qumran 'lacks any uniqueness.' The latest research joins a growing school of thought attempting to explode the 'Qumran myth' by stating that not only did the residents of Qumran live lives of comfort, but they did not write the scrolls at all."

The second cluster of explanations refers to the external circumstances of seemingly endless intrigue, conspiracy, and scandal surrounding the scrolls. Several factors deserve mention and attention in this connection.

To begin with, there are the quite fantastic cloak-and-dagger stories about the details surrounding the discovery and acquisition of the first seven scrolls. Some of these stories have by now gained the status of canonized myths.[6] The external circumstances that strongly impacted on the study of the scrolls also included international politics in general and, in particular, two Arab–Israeli wars, those of 1948 and 1967. Between 1948 and 1967 the study of the scrolls took place mainly at the Rockefeller Museum, in Jordanian-controlled East Jerusalem, under the aegis of an international committee which was formed for this purpose and entrusted with the publication of the scrolls. Israeli and Jewish scholars had no access to this committee or to its materials. The site of Qumran likewise remained under Jordanian control and out of bounds to Israeli archaeologists. The political situation reversed in 1967 when Israel gained control of East Jerusalem and of the Rockefeller Museum, where the scrolls were stored and studied. This had slow but long-term consequences, always much in the public eye, for the manner in which the study of the scrolls was subsequently conducted and organized. Of immediate consequence, however, was the acquisition of one of the most important of the Dead Sea scrolls, the *Temple Scroll*. The events which brought the scroll to light and led to its chase and purchase by Yadin occurred as the Six Day War was being waged and during its immediate aftermath.[7]

---

6   For a wonderful first-person narration of the entire story see Yadin, 1992a, pp. 15–52. A major myth creator regarding these stories was of course Wilson, 1969. See esp. the chapters "The Metropolitan Samuel" (pp. 3–21) and "General Yadin" (pp. 112–120).

7   "On June 7, 1967, the Israeli army captured the Old City of Jerusalem and Bethlehem. The next day Yadin [who was then serving as military advisor to the prime minister] arranged for an army officer to go to the Bethlehem dealer's home and claim the scroll he had learned about six years earlier from Mr. Z. That night, the delighted archaeologist held the *Temple Scroll* in his hands for the first time. It turned out to be the longest relatively intact Dead Sea scroll ever discovered, nearly twenty-seven feet long" (Shanks, 1992a, p. 119). See also Yadin's own, longer account, where he argues that the *Temple Scroll* is the Essene Torah, "equal in importance to the traditional Torah" (Yadin, 1992b, esp. pp. 88–93).

Independent of the political issues there were also charged religious and denominational ones. These had mostly to do with allegations, never proven, of suppression of scrolls-related material by the Vatican.[8] But perhaps best known among the extracurricular circumstances surrounding the scrolls research that contributed to the extraordinary interest in it were the highly publicized crises involving the issue of monopoly over the scrolls and the charges concerning delays in their publication. The monopoly crisis came to a head and made frequent headline news in the late 1980s. It was mostly resolved with the announcement by the director of the Huntington Library in Pasadena, California, on September 1991, that the library would make available to everyone the complete set of negatives of the scrolls deposited there.[9] As for publication, the mammoth task of full publication of all the scroll fragments is now finally on the verge of completion, in forty volumes in the series Discoveries in the Judaean Desert (DJD).

Finally, there is an additional external circumstance which surely contributed to the public-relations success of the field. It is the charisma of some of its early scholars, notably Sukenik, Yadin, and de Vaux, about whom more will be said later.[10] To this list one must also add the unique status of Edmund Wilson, the influence of whose early *New Yorker* articles and best-selling book on the scrolls cannot be overestimated. The end result of all of these factors is an unusual mix of Christianity, collusion, and charisma that is evidently highly potent. For more than five decades now, it has proven irresistible to scholars and to the general public alike.[11]

---

8   The thesis that the Vatican has suppressed the Dead Sea Scrolls for fear that they would undermine Christian doctrine is elaborated by Baigent and Leigh, 1991. For more discussion of this, see Shanks, 1992b and also Fitzmyer, 1992, pp. 167–169.

9   For a highly detailed (and partisan) account of the struggle for access to the scrolls see Golb, 1995, chapter 8 (pp. 217–247), entitled "Power Politics and the Collapse of the Scroll Monopoly."

10 Yadin's generally accepted reputation has been challenged by Ben-Yehuda (2002), who claims that in his account of Masada, Yadin was "intentionally engaging in deception" and that he misused his charisma and scholarly authority when he lent credibility to "a fabricated and mostly factless tale."

11 Edmund Wilson quotes eminent scholar David Flusser's "terrific pun" on *megillot,* the Hebrew word for scrolls: *"Tout le monde est megillotmane!"* (Wilson, 1969, p. 83.)

THE PROBLEM OF IDENTIFICATION

From the outset, one of the major questions in the field of scroll research, if not the major one, has been that of identifying the authors of the scrolls.[12] Ideally, of course, to identify an author is to be able to say who he or she is, to give a name. Meaningful identification of authors is sometimes possible even if no specific names can be named. While the identities of authors of ancient manuscripts are often hard to come by, in the case of the Dead Sea scrolls the task of establishing the authors' identity seemed particularly hopeless. Cryptic and elusive as regards reference to any contemporary event or person, the scrolls seem intent on concealing who they belonged to and who wrote them. Yet, upon glancing at the first major scrolls found in Cave 1, the scholars involved had no hesitation in pronouncing that these texts clearly belonged to an esoteric group – to a sect. And so the problem of identifying the authors of the Dead Sea scrolls was from the start framed as a problem of identifying a sect.

What does this mean, "to identify a sect"? I shall postpone discussing the pertinent question of why we should wish to identify a group as a sect rather than, say, as a party or movement, and take it up in Chapter Three. In principle, identifying a sect could mean one of two things. You may identify a sect by listing its distinct characteristics, by describing its beliefs and its way of life. Having done this, you may proceed to give it a name – for example, the Qumran Community or the Dead Sea Sect. Alternatively, you may identify a sect by identifying it with an already known one, for example, the Essenes. To identify in the first sense is to *define*, to identify in the second sense is to *equate*. To this, too, I shall return.

---

12 Clearly, the other major question was that of dating the scrolls. After the original suspicions of forgery were laid to rest, there emerged a consensus view that dates the sect to the Second Temple period, comprising the Hasmonean and the early Roman periods and ending in 68 CE. Initial challenges to this view came from several quarters. Some scholars maintained a late first-century beginning date, to allow for identifying the Qumran sect with the Zealots (Roth, Driver) or with early Christians (Teicher). Others maintained that the scrolls belong to the medieval Karaites (Zeitlin). The consensus on the dating seems secured, however, by the combination of archaeological evidence, carbon-14 tests (conducted on the cloth wrappings of the scrolls from Cave 1 as well as on some of the scrolls themselves), and paleography.

In the case of the Dead Sea scrolls, as it happens, there seemed initially to have been no hesitation between these options. With remarkable speed, on the strength of the first scrutiny of just a few columns of the scroll which later came to be referred to as the *Rule of the Community*, the document was conjectured to be Essene. And this equating hypothesis was instantly received as an authoritative pronouncement applying to all of the non-biblical documents from Cave 1, thus forming the hard core of the so-called Qumran–Essene theory which dominated the field of scrolls research ever since. The instantaneousness of the pronouncement of this equating hypothesis, as well as of its widespread adoption, is surely remarkable. But it is even more remarkable considering the fact that the appellation "Essene" occurs nowhere in the *Rule of the Community*, nor in any of the other scrolls in the entire Qumran corpus.

One of the factors that contributed to the instant entrenchment of this hypothesis was no doubt the authority of its author, the scholar–archaeologist E. L. Sukenik.[13] But at the same time it has to be acknowledged that the prima facie evidence for this identification is indeed striking. There are strong surface similarities between the descriptions of the Essenes known to us from the contemporary sources of the period and the material contained in the *Rule of the Community*. The similarities have to do with the organized way of life, doctrines, and practices of the community to which this document belonged. Quoting at length from Josephus' description of the Essenes, Yadin concludes as follows: "This description shows the evident similarity between the Essenes and the Dead Sea sect. The Essenes avoid a life of wealth, and share all belongings. They do not concentrate in one place of dwelling but live in scattered camps.... That the Essenes will

---

13 "Sukenik was the first who suggested the identification of the sect with the Essenes," writes his son, Yigael Yadin (1992a, p. 176.) Sukenik himself reports, diary style, his very first impressions from glancing at a scroll, obviously the *Rule of the Community*, which at that time (before the 1948 Arab–Jewish war broke out) was one of four still in the possession of the Syrian Metropolitan in Jerusalem: "I found in [it] a kind of book of regulations for the conduct of members of a brotherhood or sect. I incline to hypothesize that this cache of manuscripts belonged originally to the sect of the Essenes" (see Golb, 1995, p. 66: his translation from Sukenik's 1948 book in Hebrew). The four scrolls eventually made their way to New York, where they were purchased in 1954 by Yadin on behalf of the State of Israel.

do nothing without the express order of their curators, that new members are not accepted unless first going through a period of probation, is also similar to what we have learned of the Dead Sea sect. Many of the parallels are striking" (1992a, p. 182).

But scholarly reputation and strong prima facie textual evidence by themselves are insufficient to account for the hold which the dominant theory was to exert. I believe that there was an important additional factor at work here, namely, the irresistible allure of the notion that these miraculously preserved scrolls may offer us an unmediated link to the fabled Essenes. This prospect at once ignited both scholarly and popular imagination. Already Josephus Flavius, the first-century historian who is our source for most of what we know about the Essenes, was apparently aware of their potential appeal to the Hellenistic audience of his own time. He indulges in lengthy descriptions of the Essenes, describing them as peace-loving, ascetic, celibate people, strict in their observance of purity laws, sharing their property, and leading a communal life. Josephus' portrayals of the Essenes are in fact lengthier and more detailed than his descriptions of the two major, and much larger, Jewish parties (or "philosophies," as he refers to them): the Pharisees and Sadducees. The Qumran–Essene hypothesis, then, was bolstered by a powerful combination of factors not often encountered in the history of scientific theories: seemingly strong textual evidence supporting it, a reputable scientist proclaiming it, and wide-spread eagerness to believe it.

Thus it came about that the complex scientific enigma of the Dead Sea scrolls was thrust upon the world packaged from the start together with a solution. The bare initial circumstances of the discovery of ancient, cloth-wrapped manuscript scrolls inside jars in a cave in the Judaean Desert, the bare initial facts of their biblical and non-biblical contents, and the preliminary archaeological finds at the site of Khirbet Qumran (of which more later) were all woven together from the start into an explanatory narrative. And a compelling and attractive one it was. The essential elements of the story as they emerged were these: The scrolls found in the caves belonged to a library of a single and singular group of people. The group is identified as the Essenes known to us from the writings of three first-century authors – Josephus Flavius, Philo of Alexandria, and Pliny the

Elder. The Essenes' center for more than 150 years was the compound of Qumran. There they wrote and copied their scrolls until they hurriedly hid them away for safety in a number of nearby caves, at the approach of the Roman Tenth Legion in 68 CE.[14]

To be sure, the identification of the Qumran sect with the Essenes, which is the center-piece of the reigning theory, did not go unchallenged in the early years. Nor is it left unchallenged today. But there are important differences between the nature of the challenges then and now. Mostly they have to do with the observation that during the first decade of scrolls research the alternative proposals to the Qumran–Essene hypothesis consisted, basically, of a long series of alternative equating-identifications for the Qumran sect. There is in fact no group, movement, party, or sect known from antiquity with which the Qumran sect has not been identified by one scholar or another. "Every conceivable – and inconceivable – sect, sub-sect and combination of sects has been suggested to identify the Dead Sea sect" (Sussmann, 1994, p. 192).[15] Among them are the Sadducees, Pharisees, Hasidim (a pietistic group), Zealots, Ebionites, Karaites, early Christians, and more. These hypotheses had to be dealt with by scholars of the mainstream view,[16] but they were not considered threatening. Nowadays, in contrast, some of the challenges to the dominant theory come from within the mainstream. These challenges, based as they are on the cumulative results of five decades of research, are of a more subtle nature, and they have the effect of putting the proponents of the dominant theory somewhat on the defensive.

In what follows I aim to expose in detail the nature of the reasoning behind the dominant theory. This will turn out to yield a grid within which

---

14 The influential, mainstream exponents of this view during the 1950s, apart from Sukenik, de Vaux, and Yadin, included Frank M. Cross, Millar Burrows, and Andre Dupont-Sommer. Golb (1995, at pp. 12–13) is a lone voice disputing the consensus reasoning regarding the year 68 CE as the end point. He puts the capture of Qumran later, after the fall of Jerusalem, possibly in 73 CE.

15 See also Yadin, 1992a, p. 173.

16 For example, see de Vaux's lengthy treatment (1973, pp. 117–126) of the Zealot hypotheses put forward by Roth and Driver. Also, see his summary dismissal of Teicher's Judeo–Christian hypothesis, North's Sadducees, and Rabin's Pharisees (pp. 126–128).

all the challenges to the theory can be located in their appropriate place and, moreover, can be accorded their appropriate relative weight.

THE EMERGENCE OF THE QUMRAN–ESSENE HYPOTHESIS

Yadin

One of the first book-length expositions about the scrolls was written by Sukenik's son Yigael Yadin (1992a).[17] Yadin was a scholar and an archaeologist, like his father, but also a military general in the Israeli army and, later in life, an active politician. A prominent proponent of the Qumran–Essene hypothesis, Yadin puts off discussing the "major problem" of identifying the authors of the scrolls to the last section of his book. "Who were the people who lived in the neighborhood of Khirbet Qumran, [used the communal building in the ruins,] wrote the scrolls and hid them in the caves?" he asked (1992a, p. 173; the words inside the square parenthesis occur in the original Hebrew edition of Yadin's book but were omitted in the English edition).

Yadin duly mentions the fact that researchers disagree about the solution to the problem of identification, implicitly accepting it as an equating problem: "There is hardly a sect in Judaism or early Christianity which has not already been identified with the sect of the scrolls" (ibid.). He proceeds to elicit from the texts of the scrolls themselves a list of distinctive items regarding the beliefs, political views, and social organization of the Qumran sect.

Here, in brief headline style, are the main conclusions drawn by Yadin from the texts of the scrolls (ibid., pp. 173–176):

- The sect is opposed to the unification of the priesthood and the kingship in one person. It believed, rather, in two anointed figures, a lay leader from the House of David and a religious head descending from Aaron;

17 Other writers whose books about the scrolls appeared in the 1950s (in addition to those mentioned in n. 14 above) include John Allegro, Edmund Wilson, and Geza Vermes).

• The sect kept a solar calendar of three hundred and sixty four days, as opposed to the lunar calendar in use in Jerusalem;

• The sect was most orthodox in observance of the Law of Moses and its interpretation of the Torah laws was stricter than was customary in Jerusalem;

• Within the sect there were groups whose members remained celibate;

• The sect attached particular importance to cleanliness and purity of soul and body;

• The sect believed in predestination and in angels;

• While preparing for the war of the Sons of Light against the Sons of Darkness at the end of time, the sect opposed warfare during their time;

• The sect rejected city life;

• The sect ("as far as concerned the Dead Sea area") led a communal life of modesty and fanatical orthodoxy devoid of individual possessions, its members ate together with the priest officiating, they had special rules for promotion and demotion in seniority and during ceremonies they dressed according to seniority, they inflicted severe punishments on transgressors of all kinds, they spent their days studying the Bible and they "waited patiently for the day of vengeance against all enemies of the Sons of Light."

From this list one may form the impression that Yadin opted for a change of strategy regarding the identification of the Dead Sea sect, namely, from equating-identification to defining-identification. But following this detailed list he continues to juxtapose to it a no less detailed enumeration of the characteristics of the Essenes, drawn from the writings of the three classical sources, Josephus, Philo, and Pliny (pp. 176–185). The point of the exercise, as Yadin puts it, is to let the reader "judge the resemblance for himself" (p. 177). In other words, Yadin leads his readers to draw their own equating-identification conclusion on the basis of this comparison of the two lists of items. But not without a little help from the author:

> We therefore have before us two alternative conclusions: either the sect of the Scrolls is none other than the Essenes themselves; or it

was a sect which resembled the Essenes in almost every respect, its dwelling place, its organization, its customs (p. 186).

And if one seems to detect ever so slight a note of irony in this formulation, here is how Frank Moore Cross, another major pillar of the dominant theory, put the very same point (1992, p. 25):

> The scholar who would "exercise caution" in identifying the sect of Qumran with the Essenes places himself in an astonishing position. He must suggest seriously that *two* major parties formed communalistic religious communities in the same district of the Dead Sea and lived together in effect for two centuries, holding similar bizarre views, performing similar or rather identical lustrations, ritual meals, and ceremonies.
>
> He must suppose that one [the Essenes], carefully described by classical authors, disappeared without leaving building remains or even potsherds behind; the other [the inhabitants of Qumran], systematically ignored by the classical authors, left extensive ruins, and indeed a great library. I prefer to be reckless and flatly identify the men of Qumran with their perennial houseguests, the Essenes.[18]

In this remarkable and often quoted passage Cross, like Yadin, presupposes as a matter of course that the site of Qumran was indeed inhabited by a communal religious sect and that the library deposited in the caves belonged to it. He heaps scorn on the very idea that the identity between this sect and the Essenes can be doubted.

Let us turn our attention now to an indisputable *locus classicus* where this web of assumptions and identifications is explicitly presented, rather than sarcastically presupposed or condescendingly intimated.

---

18 For a critical discussion of this passage, as well as a reference to VanderKam in this context, see Golb, 1995, pp. 89–90 (including the footnote on p. 90). For a much more recent defense of identifying the sectarians with the Essenes, also based on a comparison much like Yadin's, see VanderKam, 1992.

De Vaux

Roland de Vaux, the archaeologist of Qumran, died in 1971 before ever publishing the definitive report of his five seasons of excavations at the site. The full-length exposition of his finds and of his views is in his *Archaeology and the Dead Sea Scrolls* (1973), which is a somewhat expanded version of his 1959 Schweich Lectures at the British Academy.

De Vaux's remarks about the interplay between the study of writings and the study of ruins merit close consideration:

> In the study of the Qumran documents archaeology plays only a secondary role. But it has the advantage of supplying dates and bringing to bear certain material facts, the interpretation of which can be more objective than that of the texts, which are so often enigmatic or incomplete (p. 138).

As previously noted, a main thrust of my book is to challenge the assumption underlying this statement. I hope to show that the purportedly impeccable objectivity of the archaeologists' interpretation of material artifacts, as compared with the purportedly flawed objectivity of the scholars' interpretation of texts, should be seriously questioned. This to me is one of the most intriguing questions underlying the present study.

Still, de Vaux himself is cautious. On the specific question of identification he says that "lack of certitude hangs over all the archaeological evidence which we might be tempted to invoke in order to establish that the Qumran community was Essene in character." And he continues:

> There is nothing in the evidence to contradict such an hypothesis, but this is the only assured conclusion that we can arrive at on the basis of this evidence, and the only one which we can justifiably demand of it. The solution to the question is to be sought from the study of the texts, and not from that of the archaeological remains (p. 133).

The tenor of de Vaux's voice is scientific, measured, and guarded. He explicitly says that the onus of solving the identity riddle is on the interpreters of the texts rather than on the archaeologists, and that the most the archaeologists can do is ascertain whether or not their material finds are *compatible* with the conjectures of the texts scholars. But he does not stop there. Rather, he himself embarks upon a detailed exegesis of Pliny the Elder's text about the Essenes (*Natural History*, Book 5, 15.73, written ca. 74 CE). In this text Pliny famously describes the Essenes as a "solitary tribe" (*gens sola*) which dwells on the western shore of the Dead Sea and which "is remarkable beyond all other tribes in the whole world, as it has no women and has renounced all sexual desire, has no money, and has only palm-trees for company." De Vaux deals at some length with the various discrepancies between the description of the Essenes in Pliny's text and the image of the community that emerges from the writings and ruins of Qumran. And then he reaches his conclusion:

> It must be recognized that this particular passage in Pliny is not *in itself* decisive. But if the writings of Qumran exhibit certain points of resemblance to what is known from other sources about the Essenes, and if the ruins of Qumran correspond to what Pliny tells us about the dwelling-place of the Essenes, his evidence can be accepted as true. And this evidence in its turn serves to confirm that the community was Essene in character. This is no vicious circle, but rather an argument by convergence, culminating in that kind of certitude with which the historian of ancient times often has to content himself (p. 137; emphasis in original).

De Vaux asserts that this argument, which he calls an "argument by convergence," involves no vicious circle.

Compare de Vaux's assertion with what David Flusser writes, more recently: "In the early days of scroll research Josephus served as guide to understanding the scrolls, but nowadays the scrolls help us understand what Josephus says about the Essenes" (Flusser, 1997, p. 94). Lawrence Schiffman is even blunter: "Scholars used the material from Philo, Josephus, and Pliny as a means of interpreting the scrolls and vice versa, thus giving rise to a circular process" (Schiffman, 1994, p. 17). Some scholars write as if the three ancient sources can be "both supplemented and *corrected* by recourse to the texts discovered in the Qumran caves" (Golb, 1995, p. 50; emphasis in original).

The situation seems to be as follows: First, surface similarities are noted between the contents of the scrolls and the writings of the three ancient authors who tell of the Essenes. Then, on the basis of these similarities the scrolls are conjectured to be Essene. Next, given apparent discrepancies between the texts of the three ancient writers, on the one hand, and the scrolls, on the other, the three writers are deemed inaccurate and not very well informed. At the final step, the historical writings are supplemented and corrected in light of the scroll material.

Questions of circularity abound. Are we in Wonderland? Has a boundary been crossed between a benign, or legitimate circle and a possibly vicious, or illegitimate one? Let me proceed to examine the logic of de Vaux's "argument by convergence" in detail. As we shall see, the circle here encountered is embedded in a yet larger and thicker one.

THE LINKAGE ARGUMENT

The Weak Version

In the quoted passage de Vaux starts out with two separate observations. First, there is the resemblance between the Qumran writings and the descriptions of the Essenes by the three ancient authors. Second, there is the correspondence between the site of Qumran and Pliny's location of the Essenes. Taking these observations as two premises of an inference, de Vaux draws the conclusion that Pliny's evidence is true. Given his belief that he has indeed validly deduced this conclusion, de Vaux then takes the new conclusion to further establish, or "confirm," that the Qumran community was Essene.

Let the question of the formal logical validity of this argument not detain us here.[19] Let us remind ourselves instead of the point, often stressed in

---

19   The argument can be reconstructed roughly as follows: (a) There is resemblance between the descriptions of the community contained in the scrolls and the descriptions of the Essenes contained in the writings of Pliny (as well as the other two classical sources); (b) There is correspondence between the location of the ruins of Qumran and Pliny's description of the dwelling-place of the Essenes. Therefore: There is identity between the community described in the scrolls and the Essenes.

By way of comparison, imagine that archaeologists some two millennia from now

textbooks of logic, that even when an inference is exposed as invalid its conclusion is not thereby proved to be false. The tenuousness of the inference notwithstanding, we may still charitably try to follow the spirit of de Vaux's argument rather than his actual reasoning, and come up with a more interesting and perhaps a more coherent result.

The starting point of the reconstructed argument remains de Vaux's two observations – about the writings, on the one hand, and the ruins, on the other. The first one notes that there is broad compatibility, indeed sometimes a striking resemblance, between the contents of the scrolls found in the caves and the descriptions of the Essenes contained in the classical sources. The second notes a putative compatibility between the physical location of the ruins of Qumran and Pliny's placing of the Essene settlement. A further tacit assumption that impels the argument is that the accounts of the three classical writers, Pliny, Josephus, and Philo, are reliable.

At this point however, the reconstructed reasoning diverges from de Vaux's original one. Instead of taking these two observations as premises of an (unsuccessful) inference, let us think of them as the starting points of two chains. And let us now extend each chain by following its own logic through.

The first chain, which connects the scrolls with the three ancient authors, is to be prolonged by drawing the prima facie conclusion that the scrolls belonged to the Essenes. That is to say, the resemblance between the contents of the scrolls and the way the Essenes are described by the three first-century authors provides inductive support for the conclusion that the scrolls are Essene. Similarly the second chain, connecting the location of

---

were to make the following argument about a site on the outskirts of Moscow: (a) There is resemblance between the description of an ill-fated winter invasion by Hitler (contained in a sole surviving document discovered near the battle ruins) and Tolstoy's description of an ill-fated winter invasion by Napoleon; (b) There is correspondence between the location of the battle ruins outside Moscow and Tolstoy's description of the location of the Napoleonic battle. Therefore: There is identity between Hitler's and Napoleon's ill-fated winter invasions.

Does de Vaux's assertion that his argument culminates in "that kind of certitude" with which scholars have to content themselves, apply in this case too?

the site of Qumran with what Pliny says about the dwelling place of the Essenes, is to be prolonged by drawing the prima facie conclusion that the Essenes lived at Qumran.

The question now is how to establish a connection between these two separate chains and, in particular, between their conclusions. The conclusion of the first chain is that the scrolls are Essene and of the second that Qumran was Essene: how then can the scrolls and Qumran become directly connected? What is the nature of the missing link?

A possible link between the chains can presumably be provided by consideration of the physical proximity between the caves in which the scrolls were found and the site of Qumran. Consider the following formulation by historian Cecil Roth, to be referred to as the *proximity presumption*: "Unless there is a very strong argument against it, archaeological evidence must be interpreted within the context of the place where it was discovered" (Roth, 1964-66, pp. 81–87).[20] Since the caves in which the scrolls were found are close to the site of Qumran, the proximity presumption urges us to interpret the scrolls "within the context" of Qumran. We are urged, then, to assert that the scrolls (or at least some of them) "belonged" to Qumran, that is, they originated there and were authored by the Essene occupants of Qumran.

The following is a schematic presentation of the argument – call it the linkage argument – for the (prima facie) web of identifications which form the core of the Qumran–Essene hypothesis.

---

20   Roth refers to this as one of the "accepted canons of scholarship" (which in the terminology here used would be the same as the "accepted presumptions of scholarship"). And he goes on to explain: "If this rule is not observed, a scholar will always be at liberty to disregard as extraneous any object or ancient record which runs contrary to his preconception." (This "canon of scholarship," incidentally, was put to interesting use in the case of the Nag Hamadi Gnostic finds.) Golb quotes this passage of Roth's approvingly (1995, p. 135) in the context of the question how to interpret the fact that a distinctly sectarian Qumran text, the *Songs of the Sabbath Sacrifice*, was found at Masada as well. Ironically, the very same canon of scholarship can be put to work against Golb's own hypothesis according to which the scrolls found in the caves have no relation to the nearby site of Qumran (but were brought there from Jerusalem for safekeeping).

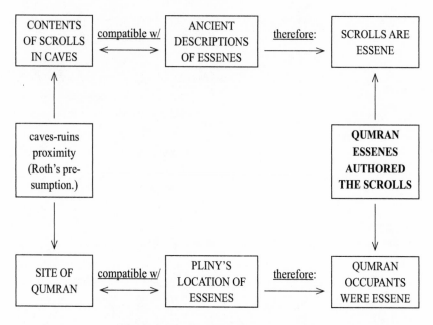

Figure 1: The Weak Linkage Argument

The first chain starts from the top left to its conclusion on the top right, and the second chain starts from the bottom left to its conclusion at the bottom right. The proximity presumption provides the vertical link, on the left-hand side, between the two starting points – the scrolls found in the caves and the site of Qumran. This link now connects the two chains, making it possible to establish the three-way connection – between the Essenes, the scrolls, and Qumran – which is what the Qumran–Essene hypothesis states. The conclusion of the linkage argument is presented on the right-hand side, as the product of the connection between the two separate conclusions of the two original chains: the Essenes who occupied the site of Qumran were the authors of (at least some of) the scrolls found in the nearby caves.

Note that this linkage argument does not rely on any of the archaeological finds at Qumran, let alone on their interpretation. The argument relates only to the location of the Qumran settlement, not to the settlement itself or to anything that was found there. Moreover, since the link connecting the two chains in this argument is a mere presumption, the argument itself is only as strong as the strength of the presumption. It establishes its conclusion only weakly and tentatively, just so long as there is no good reason for not interpreting the scrolls within the context of the site near which they were discovered. And as we shall see in the next chapter, the Qumran controversy in the last two decades revolves precisely around this point, namely about whether the scrolls can reasonably be interpreted in complete detachment from the site of Qumran and whether they can reasonably be argued to have originated elsewhere (in Jerusalem, for instance) and to have been brought to the caves merely for safekeeping. In what follows I shall reconstruct de Vaux's enterprise as an attempt to replace the weak linkage argument with a strong one.

De Vaux's Strong Version

In the concluding sentence of his book de Vaux says the following: "All that archaeology can contribute is to provide a yardstick by which to test the conclusions arrived at from the documents. But inconclusive though it may be in this role, its evidence must still not be disregarded" (1973, p. 138) One should not be misled, however, by these (and other) modest claims de Vaux makes on behalf of archaeology. In fairness it must be said that de Vaux does adhere to his own strictures, even if only up to a point. Thus he examines various theories, purporting to be based on the evidence from the scrolls material, in light of the archaeological finds, and dismisses them as not measuring up to the yardstick of archaeology.[21] But at the same time he allows his very portrayal of the archaeological finds to be strongly influenced by the contents of the literary documents – as well as, one suspects, by his wishful preconceptions.

21 For example, de Vaux examines various proposals for identifying the central scrolls figures of the Teacher of Righteousness and the Wicked Priest in light of what emerges from the archaeological evidence regarding the time frame of the establishment of the Qumran community. "It seems, therefore, that archaeology rules out any attempt to identify the Wicked Priest with Alexander Jannaeus" (p. 116), since the first installation of the site, the so-called Period Ia, is earlier than Jannaeus (103–76 BCE). Similarly, see his refutations (pp. 118–126) of Cecil Roth's and of G. R. Driver's theories that identify the occupants of Qumran as Zealots ("Driver's historical conclusions are incompatible with the most solidly established of the archaeological data" p. 124).

In other words, the use de Vaux makes of the material finds far outstrips his ideal of merely providing an objective yardstick against which to measure the textual evidence. His finds are not raw material: they are materials under interpretive description. It is because of de Vaux, after all, that the site of Qumran is so often referred to as the first monastery in the Western world.[22] And it was de Vaux who introduced the anachronistic and suggestive designation of one of the loci in the site as a "scriptorium" (a scribes' copying room in a monastery) and of another as a "refectory" (a dining hall of a religious order) – both terms carrying distinct medieval Christian connotations.

Consider the telling case regarding the periodization of Qumran. Magness believes that the sum total of the archaeological evidence suggests that the settlement at Qumran was established between 100–50 BCE. This estimate is considerably later than de Vaux's: his date for the establishment of the settlement is ca. 135 BCE. In trying to account for de Vaux's faulty assessment, Magness says the following: "I suspect that de Vaux pushed the foundation date of the settlement somewhat earlier than the evidence warrants, not only because of the coins, but because the *Damascus Document* suggests that the sect's beginnings date to 390 years after the Babylonian destruction of Jerusalem and the first Jewish Temple in 586 BCE" (Magness, 2002, p. 65).[23]

This implies the following view of de Vaux's procedure. First, on the basis of his excavations of the site of Qumran, he came up with the Qumran–Essene–scrolls hypothesis. And then, based on this hypothesis, he used the literary evidence of the scrolls – in defiance of what the archaeological material indicates (at least according to Magness' view) – in order to determine when the site was established. In other words, Magness sees de Vaux as operating within an interpretive circle, where the archaeological find, which is supposed to shed light on the literary

22 To the best of my knowledge, de Vaux himself never explicitly said this; Broshi, in contrast, maintains it all the time.

23 390 years after 586 BCE is 196 BCE. To this are added the apocryphal 20 years "before the appearance of the Teacher of Righteousness" and an additional 40 years "before the dawn of the messianic era" in order to arrive at 136 BCE as the year the sectarian settlement at Qumran was established.

evidence, is being constrained and interpreted by this literary evidence itself. De Vaux in effect is negotiating an interpretative fit in two directions simultaneously. Not only are text-based theories required to fit within the parameters of the archaeological finds, but the terms in which the archaeological data are couched are slanted by the texts. Would the terms "monastery," "scriptorium," and "refectory" be suggested by archaeologists to characterize the site of Qumran had its excavation taken place before, and not after, the discovery of the scrolls in the nearby caves? (I take up this hypothetical question in Chapter Two.)

I am now in a position to present the point of de Vaux's book within the framework of my reconstruction. De Vaux's enterprise is an attempt to provide a strong, direct, and non-presumptive connection between the two chains of the linkage argument. His archaeology characterizes the site of Qumran as a religious site, as a "motherhouse" of a religious sect, thereby supplying a direct link between the religious contents of the scrolls, on the one hand, and the ruins of Qumran, on the other. Recall that, in its weak version, the linkage argument for the Qumran–Essene hypothesis was entirely independent of the archaeological finds and that it relied solely on the presumptive proximity consideration to link the scrolls and the site. De Vaux's contribution to the linkage argument, in contrast, is in establishing a direct connection between its two chains based on his interpretation of the archaeological finds.

This connection is achieved, minimally, in virtue of the fact that according to de Vaux all the physical installations in the ruins of Qumran are compatible with what the texts tell us about the scroll community and its way of life. In his more ambitious mode, however, de Vaux offers a far stronger thesis, namely that the archaeological evidence in and of itself indicates that the site was inhabited by a monastic sect leading a communal life. At one point he says that it is the archaeological evidence which "suggests to us that this group was a religious community [which] was organized, disciplined, and observed special rites" (p. 110).

The linkage argument thus becomes a robustly closed circle. Its conclusion establishes the tightest connection among the three elements – the scrolls, the Essenes, and the site of Qumran: Qumran was a motherhouse of a religious sect; the sectarians inhabiting Qumran were the Essenes; it is in

Qumran as their center that the Essenes wrote and copied (at least a certain number of) the scrolls found in the nearby caves. De Vaux's strong linkage argument is thus a choice specimen of a hermeneutic circle in which the interpretation of material evidence is made possible by the interpretation of texts which are in turn illuminated by the material evidence.

Quite generally, a hermeneutic circle, or a "circle of understanding," refers to a situation in which, in order to understand something (say a text, a form of life, or an archaeological find), call it A, it is necessary first to understand something else, B, but the understanding of B in turn requires a prior understanding of A. For some, like Heidegger, hermeneutic circles are charmed rather than vicious. For others they are vicious, especially if they are felt to be too thin or if their diameter is too small, so to speak. For example, it may indeed feel uncomfortable if the finding of scrolls in caves near a site is taken directly to explain that some ink-wells found at that site belonged to scribes who used them to write the scrolls, while at the same time the finding of the ink-wells is taken directly to explain that the site was a scribal center. In the case of the linkage argument, however, we have a circle that connects several rich elements. It connects the interpretation and understanding of an overall extensive archaeological site with the interpretation and understanding of an entire corpus of texts, the latter corpus comprising a large number of scrolls, on the one hand, and the literary writings of three major ancient authors, on the other. The linkage argument in this sense constitutes what we might consider a "thick" circle.

The following is the schematic presentation of the strong linkage argument.

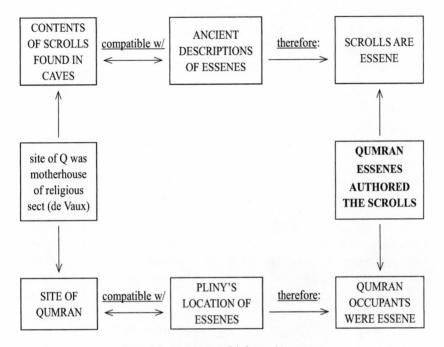

Figure 2: The Strong Linkage Argument

THE STRENGTH OF THE LINKAGE ARGUMENT

How are we to evaluate this argument? How strong is it? Where is it vulnerable? How can we decide whether the circle it involves is charmed or vicious?

The argument looks compelling. I believe that its seemingly compelling nature owes much to its gestalt. That is to say, it looks compelling because it is a closed chain in which each individual link appears to gain in strength and stature precisely because it is part of the chain: the chain curiously appears to be stronger than any of its links. Moreover, it is not only a complete circle but it is also a thick circle in that it manages to interlace three independent strands of sources: scrolls-textual, archaeological, and literary. As the individual links clink into this tightly interlocking closed chain, the mere prima facie force that each link has seems, as if by a sleight of hand, to turn conclusive.

Still, in considering the strength of the argument we have to assess the strength of each of its separate links. After all, there does seem to be some validity to the notion that a chain is only as strong as its weakest link. And as the history of Qumran Studies shows, no link in this argument has as a matter of fact been left unchallenged. I consider it an important payoff of the analysis here presented that it imposes a neat structure, or grid, on much of the huge body of Qumran scholarship, making it possible to classify its bits according to which particular link in the linkage argument they are addressing.

The Links

The link pointing to the proximity of the caves to the ruins of Qumran in the weak version of the linkage argument was already commented upon. The argument from physical proximity to causal connection has from the start been introduced as being merely presumptive. This means that when independent reasons to doubt the connection are brought forth, the presumption is rebutted. In addition to this, "proximate" is a relative, not an absolute, notion of evaluation, and while some of the eleven scrolls caves are so close to the site of Qumran as to be almost within it, others are at a distance of some two kilometers.

Another potential weakness was pointed out earlier, regarding the link that takes Pliny's description of the dwelling place of the Essenes to be referring to Qumran (bottom left). Pliny's crucial phrase is "*infra hos Engada*" meaning "under them, Engedi" or, as Rackham's translation renders it (Pliny, 1942, p. 277), "lying below the Essenes was formerly the town of Engedi." This description, taken literally, does not comfortably fit the site of Qumran. If "below" is taken to mean "lower than" or "underneath," then the problem is that the site of Qumran is more or less on the level of the Dead Sea and thus not higher than Engedi. And if it is taken to mean "to the south of," then the problem is that while Engedi is indeed located to the south of Qumran, it is very much further south, with several sites lying in between. These circumstances render the description "under them, Engedi" puzzling. (In a recent book, Hirschfeld (2004) tries to make the case that the Essenes' dwelling place was on a cliff above Engedi – where he had excavated for several seasons and found the remains of a rudimentary first-century settlement – rather than at Qumran. Magness (2005) rejects this claim.)

There are also significant challenges to the linkage argument which focus on the top-left link, that is, on the link asserting the compatibility of, or the similarities between, the texts of the caves and the writings of the three classical authors. To begin with, some discrepancies have been noted within and among the external accounts of the Essenes provided by Josephus, Philo, and Pliny.[24] This in itself would seem to weaken somewhat the link asserting compatibility between the ancient sources taken as a whole and the texts of the caves. But quite apart from this, the thrust of a good deal of scholarship over the years has been to question the Essene authorship of the scrolls and to offer alternative views.

In the early years of research, as was already pointed out, the focus of research was on trying to identify *the* Dead Sea sect with one or another of the movements, parties, or sects known or presumed to have existed during the Second Temple period in Palestine. More recently, however, given that the bulk of the scrolls and scroll fragments have by now been published, more scholars are open to the view that the documents hidden in the caves represent a wider variety of religious movements of that period and may not be the product of a single sect. (Consider: "Many of the works found at Qumran were the common heritage of Second Temple Judaism, and did not originate in, and were not confined to, Qumran sectarian circles" [Schiffman, 1992, p. 41].)

Indeed, just as inconsistencies among the three ancient literary sources are cited, so also are numerous inconsistencies, differences, and discrepancies pointed out among the various cave texts themselves. This makes it possible to argue, for example, that the texts found in the caves are the remains of various libraries belonging to various groups, possibly from Jerusalem, which were brought in haste to the Judaean Desert to be hidden in caves in time of great danger from the approaching Romans – without there being any indigenous connection between the texts and the Qumran settlement.

24 For examples, see Chapter Three, n. 9.

But the target that has remained the main focus of numerous challenges to the linkage argument throughout the years is the link supplied by de Vaux's archaeological work. As we saw, it is precisely his work which interprets the site of Qumran as the motherhouse of a communal, celibate, and ascetic religious sect. Many aspects of the site were subjected to critical scrutiny in recent years. Let me briefly mention here the more outstanding ones; I shall have occasion in Chapter Two to return to some of them in greater detail:

- The fortification of the Qumran tower and the signs of a battle being fought around it. (Was not Qumran possibly a military outpost?)
- The complex system of cisterns and water channels at Qumran. (Are not some of them just installations for water storage, rather than facilities for ritual bathing as claimed by de Vaux?)
- The furniture of the so-called scriptorium. (Are not the plastered structures found in this room perhaps the remains of dining couches running along the walls of a triclinium fit for a luxurious villa, rather than the remains of low writing tables used by scrolls-copying scribes, as suggested by de Vaux?)
- The pottery assemblage. (Is it as distinctive as it is claimed to be?)
- The finds of precious glass. (While largely ignored by de Vaux, might this not be indicative of some affluence incompatible with the ascetic character of the Essene community?)
- The composition of the cemetery. (How are the remains of females found there to be squared with the postulated celibacy of the community?)
- The nature of the industrial workshops. (What do they tell us about the nature of the Qumran settlement?).

As a result of these challenges, several scholars have offered alternative theories for the interpretation of the Qumran settlement. Among them: a fortress, a country villa (*"villa rustica"*), an industrial plant, an inn ("caravanserai"), and an agricultural manor house.[25] These alternative

---

25   Fortress: Golb, 1995; country villa: Donceel & Donceel-Voûte, 1994; industrial plant: Patrich, 1994; inn: Crown and Cansdale, 1994; agricultural manor house: Hirschfeld, 2003b. In 2004, Hirschfeld conjectures that Qumran was a "field fort and a road station" in the Hasmonean period and a manor house in the Herodian period.

interpretations typically aim to sever altogether the connection between the Qumran site and the scrolls.

Resilience and Consilience

As we have seen, no link of the linkage argument remains unchallenged. At the same time, though, no link has decidedly been broken. The Essene authorship of the scrolls remains a matter of ongoing scholarship and controversy. Pliny's reference to the geographic location of the site remains inconclusive. The consideration in favor of a causal connection between the site and the scrolls prevails in the absence of weightier considerations to the contrary. And finally, not one of the alternative archaeological interpretations offered for the site of Qumran, imaginative and partially persuasive as any of them may appear to be, is accepted as compelling by the community of scholars. Indeed, it seems that the alternative theories remain mostly one-proponent theories. So, while battered as regards its individual links, the linkage argument shows remarkable resilience as regards the chain taken as a whole. Such resilience calls for some reflection and explanation.

The resilience of the linkage argument seems to gain from the consideration that two notions of truth appear to be at work here rather than one. With regard to each individual link, the tendency is to apply the standards of a *correspondence* theory of truth: each link is confronted in isolation with the available evidence and data, and, as we saw, it is found wanting, in one respect or another. But so long as none of the links actually breaks down, we turn our attention back to the chain as a whole. And with regard to the closed chain as a whole we seem to apply the standards of a *coherence* theory of truth: we are impressed with the fact that it is a tightly interlocking interpretative circle, which manages to braid together the textual material from the scrolls, the ancient literary sources, and the archaeological data.

More insight into the resilience of the linkage argument might be gained from a methodological consideration. We seem to have here a situation similar to what W. Whewell refers to as a *consilience of inductions*. Schematically put, this is what it is about. Suppose that we consider two independent conjectures, each independently supported by its own set of evidence. Suppose further that the two conjectures can be shown to be derivable from one and the same overarching hypothesis. The point about consilience is that each of the two conjectures is now judged more probable than it was before: as consequences of the same overarching hypothesis, each of them derives additional support, indirectly, from the evidence in favor of the other (Kneale, 1963, pp. 106–110).

Let us try to apply this rough understanding of consilience to the case in hand. We have two independent conjectures, one concerning the scrolls and the other concerning the site. Spelled out, the conjectures are, first, that the scrolls are sectarian, namely, that they belong to and reflect the way of life of an active religious sect; and second, that Qumran was a center in which a communal and ritualized way of life was practiced. The evidence for the first conjecture comes from the contents of the scrolls. The evidence for the second conjecture comes from the excavation of the site (or, at any rate, from the excavation of the site as interpreted by de Vaux). These two sets of evidential considerations are supposed to be independent of one another.

Now there is an overarching hypothesis from which both conjectures follow, namely the Essene connection that originates from the historical sources: the site of Qumran was an Essene center where the Essenes wrote the scrolls. According to the doctrine of consilience, if each of the two conjectures formulated above is derivable from the overarching hypothesis, then each of these conjectures gains probative strength from the evidence supporting the other conjecture. Specifically, evidence regarding the sectarian nature of the scrolls now turns out, on purely methodological grounds, to augment de Vaux's interpretation of the archaeological finds at Qumran. It thus comes about that evidence in favor of either of the two conjectures, which initially was merely considered to be *compatible* with the other, is turned into *supportive* evidence for that other conjecture, due to the existence of the overarching hypothesis from which both are derivable.

The machinery of the consilience of inductions has thus been shown to apply to the Qumran–Essene argument. The point of this methodological detour was to provide us with a further explanation of the intuitively felt resilience of the argument. But of course one crucial caveat has to be borne in mind: the consilience consideration only works if the sets of evidence supporting our two conjectures are indeed independent of each other. That is to say, consilience applies to the Qumran–Essene argument only if de Vaux's conjecture that Qumran was a center in which a communal and ritualized way of life was practiced, can be supported exclusively by the archaeological evidence, completely independently of any scrolls-related evidence. This caveat remains a moot point, to which I shall return in Chapter Two.

Elasticity and Co-optation

An additional aspect contributing to the resilience of the Qumran–Essene hypothesis is its elasticity. While the linkage argument was never shown to break, the constant attacks on the Qumran–Essene theory which it supports have not failed to make an impact on it. The variety of alternatives proposed, even if none has gained widespread adherence, had their influence too. The theory has, in other words, undergone transformations over the years – invisible perhaps to some, quite noticeable to others. It is thus somewhat misleading to say about the Qumran–Essene theory that it has retained its dominance throughout these five decades, because the "it" that has retained its dominance has not quite retained its identity.

It may not be entirely tongue-in-cheek to suggest that, quite apart from the issue of the sectarian nature of the Qumran dwellers, there is also an issue of the sectarian attitudes of some Qumran researchers. The ideological, religious, and emotional stakes in the scrolls seem to be so high that, in the eyes of the mainstream scholars, anyone who thinks differently is not just mistaken but a deviant, if not a heretic. It has become supremely important to the mainstream scholars over the years to remain loyal and to be seen as remaining loyal to the consensus theory. And so, while not quite admitting it, they seem to have been engaged in co-optation. Their favorite hypothesis has gradually co-opted elements from various challenges to it. At the same time, they kept insisting that it has remained "the same hypothesis." In this they exemplify a phenomenon which has its parallels in the history of religion and may be referred to as *phonetic fanaticism*: the stubborn belief that by fanatically adhering to the same phonetic name or formula you may go on refusing to acknowledge the changes its meaning has undergone.[26]

26   For more on phonetic fanaticism see Ullmann-Margalit and Margalit, 1992.

Indeed, to be able to list the conditions of identity of a scientific hypothesis which is subtly being re-described may turn out to be a tricky task. It may be an even trickier task than to be able to list the conditions of identity of, say, a sectarian group – such as the Essenes.

The claim about the theory being subtly re-described needs to be substantiated. I shall now present a brief sketch of the contours of what I consider two such instances of substantiation. They relate to two major components of the Qumran–Essene theory. The first instance concerns the identity of the Essenes, and the second concerns the composition of the Qumran library.

Who Were the Essenes?

For a long time it has been felt by many Qumran researchers that the question of the identification of the Qumran community will have to await the interpretation of *Miqsat Ma'ase ha-Torah*, or MMT. This major scroll was finally published in 1994 by Qimron and Strugnell. It has a large halakhic component, and it turns out that the Jewish law contained in it is generally recognized as Sadducean. That is to say, it accords with the *halakhah* explicitly described by the rabbinic sources as Sadducean. Does this observation mean that the Dead Sea sectarians were Sadducees? Can this observation still be reconciled with the conviction that the Dead Sea sectarians were Essenes?

In a thorough study of this scroll Yaacob Sussmann (1994)[27] relates this puzzle to another relevant riddle – the total absence of the term "Essenes" not only from the Dead Sea Scrolls corpus but also from the entire rabbinic literature. (Instead, the Talmudic sources – but no others at all – speak of Boethusians, or *baytusim*.) In an attempt to solve both puzzles Sussmann embarks upon an investigation of the usage of the terms in the varied sources, in the context of studying the major religious parties of the Second Temple period. He reminds us that the divisions between Pharisees and

---

27 Originally read as a paper in 1987 at a symposium in Jerusalem, it was published in its proceedings (Broshi et al., 1992). It also appeared, with extensive documentation, in *Tarbiz* 59 (1989–90), pp. 11–76 (Hebrew), and was subsequently reproduced in English (without the extensive documentation but with a short 1993 postscript) as Appendix 1 in Qimron and Strugnell, 1994.

Sadducees had social and political dimensions in addition to the well-known religious and halakhic ones. This observation, it turns out, provides a key to the solution Sussmann offers to the puzzles. Sadducean *halakhah* was followed, as he says, "not only by the Sadducean aristocrats...but also by popular classes and fanatical religious sects" such as the Essenes (p. 194).[28]

Regarding the Dead Sea sect, Sussmann concludes that it was a spiritual and separatist sect. The sectarians found themselves "compelled to separate both from the Temple and the majority of the people" (p. 199) and turn to the desert. Religiously they adhered to Sadducean *halakhah*, but socially and politically they were bitterly opposed to the Sadducees. Indeed, this sect, he says, "waged a dual battle" (p. 194). They struggled socially against the Sadducean aristocracy, while at the same time waging a fierce religious and halakhic battle against the Pharisees.

The other key observation here is that ultimately, as the Sadduceans vanished from the stage of history, the halakhic writings known to us today reflect a Pharisaic bias. This bias tends to license the lumping together of all sects considered deviant by the Pharisees, and referring to them collectively and dismissively as "Sadducees." This is particularly true of the Pharisaic attitude toward the "Boethians" – most likely, according to Sussmann, the Pharisaic appellation for the sect of the Essenes.

In the final outcome, Sussmann combines his observations to conclude that the group whose sectarian writings were found in the Qumran caves were indeed the Essenes. But this identification now comes closer to the defining sense of identifying than to its equating sense (see pp. 32–36 above). This identifying hypothesis is now backed by a revised understanding of the sect of the Essenes, taking into account the full range of halakhic, religious, social, and political points of view. Consequently, the Qumran–Essene hypothesis, as enunciated by present-day scholars, cannot be taken as quite identical to the same-sounding hypothesis of some

---

28 Compare: "MMT revolutionizes the question of Qumran origins and requires us to consider the entire Essene hypothesis. It shows beyond question that either the sect was not Essene, but was Sadducean, or that the Essene movement must be totally redefined as having emerged out of Sadducean beginnings" (Schiffman, 1992, p. 42).

four decades ago. Whether or not this theory commands the adherence of all scholars in the field, the present-day theory is the product of a newly evolved understanding of what the term "Essenes" stands for.

The Composition of the Qumran Library

Let me now turn to the second instance meant to substantiate my claim about the elasticity of the Qumran–Essene theory and the re-description it has undergone over the years.

Recall that one strand of arguments against the Qumran–Essene hypothesis denies the connection between the Qumran compound and the texts found in the caves. Based on a variety of considerations, these arguments contend that the scrolls originated in Jerusalem: one variant maintains that the corpus of writings found in the caves formed part of the Temple library (Rengstorf, 1963), and another – that it was the remnant of a large number of private Jerusalem libraries (Golb, 1995).[29]

Initially, the scroll corpus was believed to divide into three categories: first, biblical texts (covering some part of every book of the Hebrew Old Testament except the Book of Esther); second, sectarian writings, describing the teachings, beliefs, rules, and way of life of the Qumran community; and third, so-called apocryphal and pseudo-epigraphic writings (that is, non-canonical Jewish writings composed between mid-second century BCE and the end of the first century CE). Bolstering this division was the fortuitous fact that the first seven scrolls found in Cave 1 constituted a brilliant sample of these three groups of texts.[30] In recent years, however,

---

29 There is in fact controversy as to whether or not there were libraries in Jerusalem during the Second Temple period. See Haran, 1993 and Shavit, 1994. Broshi claims that "not until the Middle Ages would Judaism be liberal enough to have libraries. Jerusalem certainly did not have libraries and the Temple must have kept no more than a collection of model texts of the Hebrew Bible for the use of copyists" (Broshi, 2004a, p. 761).

30 Cave 1 yielded two central biblical scrolls (*Isaiah 1* and *2*), one apocryphal work (the Aramaic *Genesis Apocryphon*), and four major sectarian works (*Rule of the Community*, also referred to as the *Manual of Discipline*, the *War Scroll*, also referred to as the *Scroll of the War of the Sons of Light against the Sons of Darkness*, the *Thanksgiving Hymns*, and the scriptural commentary known as *Pesher Habakkuk*). What would the nature of Qumran studies have been like had Cave 4, with its many

as the task of deciphering and publishing the entire Qumran library is nearing its completion, a different assessment appears to replace the initial one. Gradually, there is growing recognition that the sectarian texts form a smaller proportion of the entire corpus than had previously been assumed, and that the sectarian texts themselves exhibit much more diversity than had initially been realized. It also becomes increasingly evident that many scrolls fragments belong to texts whose initial relegation to the sectarian group of texts can no longer be sustained. Consequently, the consensus view regarding the composition of the Qumran library is nowadays the product of a nearly imperceptible process of re-description.

For example, in his 1994 semi-popular book, Lawrence Schiffman describes the Qumran library as comprising the following three categories of documents: biblical manuscripts, sectarian manuscripts, and a heterogeneous third category of "non-sectarian" manuscripts. The latter, says Schiffman, "were part of the literary heritage of those who formed the sect or that were composed by similar groups. They were composed outside the sectarian center and brought there, although some of them may have been copied there" (ibid., p. 33). This formulation neatly illustrates the elasticity of the consensus view. It retains the old notion of a sectarian center and it even echoes the controversial notion of a scriptorium for the copying of scrolls. At the same time it seamlessly weaves these consensual notions together with the challenging newer one of a heterogeneous literary heritage brought to Qumran from the outside.[31]

Similarly, in the official catalogue of the scrolls exhibition that traveled in the United States in 1993 there is an endorsement of the view that "a great many documents found in the caves of Qumran came from other

---

thousands of small fragments, rather than Cave 1 been discovered first? What would the leading hypothesis about the origin of the scrolls have looked like? These remain hypothetical questions that invite imaginative speculation but cannot be settled. (Norman Golb offers his own answer to these questions. He believes that his theory about the scrolls "would have been arrived at by scholars both naturally and inevitably, if only the actual order of discoveries had been *reversed*": 1995, p. 149.)

31 Revealingly, Golb's name is never mentioned in Schiffman's book – not in the text and not even in the bibliography. Does this not illustrate sectarian attitudes among the mainstream Qumran scholars?

places." That is to say, it is now no longer a sharp matter of either–or: *either* all the documents found in the caves belonged to the sect living at Qumran, and were possibly even composed and copied by the Qumran sectarians – *or* else Qumran was no sectarian center at all, and all the documents found in the caves were brought to them from Jerusalem for hiding.

The examination of the Qumran–Essene theory offered in this chapter has underscored the fuzziness of the distinction between hard facts and soft facts. Purportedly "objective," the hard, material facts of archaeology were shown to be not significantly less dependent on interpretation and personal perspective than the soft, "incomplete" facts of textual interpretation. In the next chapter I shall further expound on this theme. Center stage in this chapter, however, was occupied by a grand interpretive circle. Tracing the circular structure of the dominant theory underlying Qumran studies, I sought to bring out the peculiar power of this circle. The theme of circularity too will feature in the next chapter.

The Qumran–Essene theory and the linkage argument that supports it have been, and still are, subjected to manifold challenges. The theory may have lost some of the headiness and the air of obviousness it had in the early years. Yet none of the challenges is generally recognized to have broken any of the links of the argument. At the same time, however, I argued that the theory has gradually found its ingenious ways to co-opt some aspects of these challenges. Subtly thus re-described, it endures: in one version or another, the Qumran–Essene hypothesis retains its status as the reigning consensus in Qumran Studies.

The Essene connection, whose appeal was already appreciated by Josephus in the first century, seems capable of casting a powerful spell – religious, romantic, and social-utopian – to this day. The cognitive questions relating to the strength of the hermeneutic circle involved or to the elasticity of the dominant theory notwithstanding, an emotive aspect asserts itself forcefully: none of the alternatives to the Qumran–Essene theory can rival its attractiveness.

CHAPTER TWO

A Hard Look at "Hard Facts":
The Archaeology of Qumran

THE FANTASY

The Chain of Events

The Dead Sea scrolls were found in eleven caves that are near a site known by its Arab name, Khirbet Qumran. The ruins at the site of Qumran proved rich in non-scroll artifacts. So did the nearby caves. The study of these artifacts was expected to provide answers to a variety of basic questions: When was the site occupied? What was the nature of the settlement at Qumran? Who inhabited the site? How many inhabitants were there? What other sites, if any, are comparable to Qumran and what can be learned from the comparison? Above all, of course, the archaeologists who studied the ruins and the finds they contained were expected to shed light on the possible connection between the site of Qumran and the scrolls found in the caves.

When considering the archaeological finds of Qumran as well as the expectations from the archaeologists, one central fact has to be borne in mind: the detailed excavation of the site was undertaken only after the first caches of scrolls had been found. To be sure, already in the nineteenth century explorers noted the existence of ancient ruins at Qumran. Later, descriptions of the site from 1903 (Masterman), 1914 (Dalman), and 1940 (Avi-Yonah, who relied on Dalman)[1], surmised that the site served as a

---

1   E. W. G. Masterman, "Notes on Some Ruins and a Rock-Cut Aqueduct on the Wadi Kumran," *PEFQSt* (1903), p. 265 (reference from Hirschfeld, 2003b, p. 8); G. Dalman, *Palästina Jahrbuch des deutschen evangelischen Instituts für Altertumswissenschaft*

fortress, one of several known ancient military outposts in the Judaean Desert. In hindsight one can only lament that the ruins of Qumran had not been excavated before the discovery of the scrolls and completely independently of this discovery. Still, it is both intriguing and legitimate to speculate on the possible results of such an excavation.

In her comprehensive study of the archaeology of Qumran, Jodi Magness asserts that "archaeology establishes the connection between the scrolls in the caves and the settlement at Qumran" (2002, p. 13). She also addresses the question whether Qumran would be interpreted as a sectarian settlement had the Dead Sea scrolls not been found. Her answer is candid and quite clear: "No, we would probably not interpret Qumran as a sectarian settlement without the scrolls."[2] But she complains of the question and doubts its legitimacy. "Why would we want to disregard the evidence of the scrolls?...Qumran provides a unique opportunity to use archaeological evidence combined with the information from ancient historical sources and scrolls to reconstruct and understand the life of a community" (ibid.).

It would indeed make no sense to disregard the evidence of the scrolls. Philosophers of science have articulated a principle of total evidence, to the effect that a rational person should believe the hypothesis best supported by all available relevant evidence. More precisely, the principle enjoins us to believe the hypothesis supported by the totality of evidence available to us at a given time, to the degree to which this evidence supports the

---

des heiligen Landes 10 (1914), pp. 9–10; M. Avi-Yonah, Map of Roman Palestine, 2nd ed. (Jerusalem 1940) (references from Golb, 1995).

2   Magness continues: "Although I doubt we would interpret it as a villa or fortress either. I think it would be an anomalous site because it has too many features that are unparalleled at other sites" (2002, p. 13). I shall discuss later the features that make the site anomalous. Still, I note that Magness does not attempt to speculate on what a probable interpretation of the site would be had the scrolls not been found. More recently Magness has once again returned to this question (2005), observing that "Without the scrolls the archaeological remains are ambiguous enough to support a variety of possible interpretations – that Qumran is a villa, manor house, fort, commercial entrepot, pottery manufacturing center, and so on.... Denying any connection between Qumran and the scrolls automatically creates ambiguity." James Tabor (2005) argues that even without the scrolls the archaeological verdict on the site would be that it was a center of a religious community.

hypothesis at that time (Carnap, 1962, pp. 211ff.).[3] A piece of evidence is relevant to a hypothesis if it affects the probability that the hypothesis is true. Evidence that neither increases nor decreases the probability of a given hypothesis is considered irrelevant to that hypothesis.

But it is precisely the issue of relevance that is raised here. Do we know that the scrolls are intrinsically related to the site of Qumran? Do we have independent evidence that the scrolls are connected to Qumran? It is right to offer an interpretation of the site in light of the scrolls. But it is also right to ponder the interpretation of the material findings of the ruins independently of the textual information of the scrolls, and to ask just how far, and in what direction, this could take us.

At the end of her chapter on the pottery and architecture of Qumran Magness asserts:

> I hope that this chapter has clarified why the highly-publicized alternative interpretations of Qumran are not supported by the archaeological evidence. In the following chapters we shall examine the peculiar features of Qumran in light of the information provided by the scrolls and our ancient sources (2002, p. 100).

There is a strategy here. It comes in two stages. The first stage consists of establishing, solely on the basis of the material findings of architecture and pottery, that the sectarian interpretation of the site is the only one consistent with this evidence. Second, given this interpretation of the site, the strategy calls for proceeding to consider the "peculiar," anomalous, or unparalleled features of Qumran and fit them in with the sectarian hypothesis. It is only at this second stage – but not at the first – that it is admissible to use the literary sources of the scrolls and of the ancient historians. The strategy is cogent. The question whether it has been, or indeed can be, successfully carried out is another matter.[4]

---

3   Carnap traces a distinguished historical pedigree for the requirement of total evidence, including Jacob Bernoulli (1713), as cited by J. M. Keynes as well as C. S. Peirce.
4   My understanding of Hirschfeld's 2003a review of Magness' 2002 book is that his critique is directed mostly at the way Magness goes about carrying out the first stage.

The strategy just spelled out relates to a procedure called *inference to the best explanation* (Harman, 1965; Vogel, 1998). Essentially it is the procedure of selecting the explanation that best explains the available data. We may, for example, make the inference that there must be a source of excessive pollution in the bay to explain why the coral reef there is dying. In order for a particular explanation to be considered "best" we have to specify what it is for an explanation, hypothesis, or theory to be better than another. The criteria cited in the literature include factors such as simplicity, unifying power, comprehensiveness, and depth. Note the following peculiarity of inferences to the best explanation. According to the canonical model of explanation (the so-called deductive-nomological model) the state of affairs that we want to explain (say, the deterioration of the coral reef) is supposed to be logically inferred from some known initial conditions (say, excessive pollution). In the inference to the best explanation, in contrast, it is the as-yet-unknown existence of the initial conditions that are being inferred – or rather posited – from the resulting state of affairs.

Inferences to the best explanation are on the whole highly suggestive and appealing. They remain controversial, however, because there remains the concern that the explanatory felicity of a hypothesis may not necessarily attest to the truth of the hypothesis: explanatory virtues like simplicity and truth do not always go together.

The Fantasy in Detail
Let us imagine for a moment that a full excavation of the site of Qumran were undertaken before the discovery of the scrolls. Here is the full-fledged fantasy.

Suppose that the archaeologists excavating the site have no special difficulty in dating the main period of occupation of the site from, roughly, early in the first century BCE to the middle of the first century CE. Yet they face a riddle. They find that the site and its artifacts lack contemporary parallels and are in many ways quite unique. Features such as the animal bone deposits, the large number of ritual baths, and the large and unusual cemetery nearby make it anomalous (Magness, 2002, p. 98 and passim). The archaeologists then reason that, based on the archaeological evidence, the interpretation of the site as a military fort must be rejected. They further reject the hypothesis that the site functioned as an industrial or agricultural installation, and also, for that matter, that it was a residential villa, an agricultural manor house, a palace, an official customs post, or an inn (a so-called "caravanserai").[5] The archaeologists conclude that the nature of the site remains enigmatic: the site cannot have functioned in any of the conventional ways known to archaeologists of that period.[6]

Now, suppose that at this point the archaeologists put forward a daring hypothesis. Suppose they maintain that the best way to provide a plausible interpretation for the enigmatic findings at the site of Qumran is to postulate the existence of a peculiar group of people that occupied the site. How delightful, if they were to go on to speculate about the nature of the group and to describe it as communitarian, ritualistic, cleanliness-obsessed, and bookish. How delightful, were the scrolls to be discovered *after* such a conjecture had been put forward; how much more striking would be the confirmation of their conjecture in such a case!

In the history of science there are precedents for the fulfillment of similar fantasies. Take, for example, the case of the planet Neptune. When this planet was still unknown, its existence was postulated in 1845 by Urbain J. J. Leverrier in France and by John C. Adams in England (independently of each other, as it happens). The conjecture was made to explain the puzzling irregularities in the motion of Uranus. In the spirit of an inference to the best explanation the scientists postulated the existence of a planet that would be an additional source of gravitational attraction acting on Uranus that would account for the aberrations in its orbit. Observations confirmed the existence of the planet the following year.

---

5   All of these suggestions have their proponents (see p. 52 above). It should be noted – perhaps emphasized – that these alternative accounts are minority views; most of them have no more that one or two adherents. They serve the intended illustrative purpose, however, irrespective of one's judgment of the probative weight or scientific value of these alternative interpretations.

6   It should be noted that in order for comparisons in archaeology to carry any weight the compared sites must belong to the same historical period and geographical zone. As Magness notes: "The more distant the comparisons are in time and space, the less likely they are to be valid" (2002, p. 90). This means that the relevant comparisons for Qumran are chiefly Judaean villas, palaces, and forts spanning roughly the Roman period of first century BCE and first century CE.

General view of rooms in the southern part of the Qumran compound
© The Israel Museum, Jerusalem / by Avraham Hai

A more pertinent analogy is the case of Solomon Schechter's discovery. In 1896 a medieval copy of an unknown document was found among the texts of the Cairo Genizah, a treasure trove of medieval Hebrew manuscripts stored in the ancient Ben Ezra Synagogue in Fustat, near Cairo, Egypt. Schechter, a Cambridge University scholar, proposed a bold existence hypothesis. He conjectured that the document was part of a medieval copy of a far older text belonging to an unknown Jewish sect of the Second-Temple era (Schechter, 1910). His conjecture received its remarkable confirmation half a century later, when several ancient copies of the very same document were found among the Dead Sea scrolls.[7] This document is now known as the *Damascus Document* (or *Damascus Covenant*).

Formation and Confirmation

This is not how things turned out with Qumran, however. The excavation of the ruins at Qumran was not undertaken until after scrolls had been found in the first few caves. Moreover, the excavation was undertaken very much *because* of the discovery of these scrolls. The proximity of the caves to the ruins and the resemblance that was noticed between some pottery items unearthed from the ruins and pottery found in the caves clearly called for further investigation. This, in itself, is unobjectionable. The motivation for undertaking a major archaeological excavation, if it is not some chance discovery, is often an external reference, literary or otherwise. This is certainly the case with most of biblical archaeology.

So there is nothing wrong or suspicious as such in excavating the ruins of Qumran in the hope of finding connections between them and the scrolls found in the nearby caves. Such an undertaking only becomes wrong or suspicious if the excavators are determined to come up with such connections, and if they know in advance just what they are. The line to be drawn, then, is between hoping to find connections and being determined to find them, between being interested in a question and having a vested

---

7   Schechter further conjectured, however, that this sect was Zadokite in its interpretation of the law (*halakhah*): this conjecture is disputed.

interest in a particular answer to it. Ultimately, this line is between open-minded archaeology and wishful archaeology.[8]

Here we encounter the distinction between the context of discovery and the context of justification (Reichenbach, 1961, p. 7) – or, as I prefer, between the contexts of formation and of confirmation. A hypothesis may be discovered, formed, or hit upon in strange and wayward ways. We are told, for example, that the idea to use mercury as a treatment against syphilis occurred to Parcelsus when he noticed one night that Mercury was the planet closest to Venus. Also, we all grow up on the story of how Newton came to think of gravitation when he saw the apple falling from a tree. A hypothesis may for that matter be dictated to us in a dream. The fact that it was dictated by an authoritative-looking figure cannot in and of itself serve to justify the hypothesis. At the same time, however, the fact that it was dictated to me by an authoritative-looking figure in my dream should not count against testing the hypothesis. The process whereby a hypothesis is arrived at may be highly subjective, and the formation of the hypothesis may involve wishful thinking or an ideological agenda. But to justify the hypothesis, or to confirm it, is another matter. The *testing* of the hypothesis must conform to criteria that are accepted by the scientific community, and it must be inter-subjective and ideology-free. It is important to bear in mind that the test must be free of ideology, not necessarily the testers.

The excavation of the site of Qumran was undertaken, as was pointed out, only after the first scrolls were found and because they were found. It was undertaken in the hope of finding a specific connection between the scrolls and the site; that is, in the hope of establishing that the occupants of the site were the authors or owners of the scrolls. Moreover, the archaeological undertaking came about after the hypothesis about the Essene origin of the scrolls had already been afloat. The hope, therefore, was even more specific: to establish that the site was Essene.

---

8 The notion of "wishful archaeology" is best exemplified – tongue in cheek – by the case of St. Helena, the mother of Emperor Constantine of Byzantium. Shortly before her death, in the fourth century, she visited the Holy Land and believed that she had located everything she set out to find, including the site of Jesus' birth, the cross on which he was crucified, the site of the burning bush at Mt. Sinai, and possibly more.

"No archaeological study can be better than the ideological assumptions which underlie the development of its argument," says a noted textbook in archaeology (Clarcke, 1968, p. xv). Whatever one may mean by assumptions "which underlie the development of an argument," in the case in hand there clearly were specific ideological assumptions that *motivated* the archaeological undertaking. But still they pertain, generally speaking, to the context of the formation of the Essene hypothesis. And as such they must be regarded as unobjectionable. Matters are different with the context of justification, or confirmation. We must now turn to consider the question, what would it take to confirm the hypothesis that the site of Qumran was Essene? What would it take to refute this hypothesis?

THE METHOD

Leaving Traces

Everything we know directly about the Essenes is gleaned from literary sources. These comprise the writings (in Greek) of Josephus Flavius and Philo of Alexandria and (in Latin) of Pliny the Elder, all three of whom were first-century figures and, as such, approximate contemporaries of the Essenes. Much of this information has to do with the Essenes' views and beliefs. An intriguing problem, therefore, is whether worldviews and religious beliefs can be connected with distinct material traces: what can the archaeologists expect a community that adheres to these particular beliefs to leave behind?

For example, the sources tell us that the Essenes were distinguished in their belief in predestination. We are also told that they believed in the immortality of the soul, had a developed doctrine of angels ("angelology"), and esteemed charity (Josephus, *War* 2 VIII 2–13: 119–161). It is not easy to think of ways in which these specific beliefs can find expression in material artifacts that eventually leave traces in the form of archaeological findings. Perhaps no amount of archaeological finds, short of written or painted documents, can be expected to corroborate, let alone prove, the hypothesis that a given site was Essene in character on the basis of these beliefs and doctrines alone.

Fortunately, the picture of the Essenes that emerges from the literary sources is richer. Whatever the discrepancies among them, they tell us not only about the Essenes' doctrinal beliefs, but also about their style of life that may well be linked to hard material findings. Thus the Essenes are portrayed as a group that led a communal life, shared communal meals, shunned luxuries, and was preoccupied with bodily purity. It is not inconceivable that these elements might leave traces behind. And, no less important, these elements may well preclude certain traces.

Given this background, we may ascertain that archaeologists should consider themselves lucky, for example, if their excavation of the site of Qumran yields the remains of a large communal dining hall or of ritual baths. The point is perhaps stronger when made in the negative. Suppose the excavation of the site yields no locus that could possibly have served as a sufficiently large communal dining hall. Or again, suppose it yields no communal baths suitable for the prescribed Jewish purification ritual. In these circumstances the idea that the site could be identified as a center of the Essene community would suffer a severe blow. Also, suppose the excavation yields traces of a rich and luxurious material culture, as reflected for example in the assemblages of pottery, glass, and coins, or in the architectural design of the compound. This, too, should give the proponents of the idea of an Essene center cause to pause.

Just how lucky would the archaeologists in search of an Essene connection be in the first case, and how severe would the blow for them be in the second? There is an asymmetry here: the blow in the case of the negative findings is in principle more significant than the support in the case of the positive findings. We must also bear in mind that in archaeology not finding something is not the same as finding that something did not exist: the use of an "argument from silence" (or an argument from absence) in archaeology is a particularly delicate and tricky affair. In an attempt to examine the logic of the archaeologists' task, I shall first explore the issue purely deductively; I shall then move on to consider it from a probabilistic point of view.

The communal dining hall ("refectory"), with an adjacent pantry.
In the background, the Dead Sea and the mountains of Moab
© The Israel Museum, Jerusalem / by Avraham Hai

Reasoning about the Traces

The way the situation has been framed so far can be represented, with simplification, by a schematic implication or "if-then" sentence. It asserts that *if* Qumran was an Essene center *then* the excavations at the site would (likely) turn up such-and-such traces – for example, a large communal dining hall, or a number of ritual baths, or only unadorned pottery, etc.

From this standpoint we can now consider two options. First, the option of negative findings: the excavations do not yield the expected traces, or they yield traces that are inconsistent with the expectations. Suppose for example that they yield a structure with no locus that can function as a dining hall, no indication of ritual baths, an abundance of luxury items, etc. In this case a valid inference can be drawn. It is that Qumran was (likely) *not* an Essene center. That is to say, in the case of clear negative findings, our hypothesis is weakened, if not refuted. On the second option, the findings are affirmative: they do include, say, a large dining hall, or a number of communal baths, etc. In this case, however, deductive formal logic does not permit us to draw any valid inference. In particular, while the affirming findings seem to lend support to the hypothesis that Qumran was an Essene center,[9] the hypothesis nevertheless does not logically follow from them.

Besides, archaeological findings are seldom unambiguous and clear-cut. They "turn out to be observations in which the nature of the observer and his intentions play a large part in which 'facts' are observed and recorded" (Clarcke, 1968, p. 21). Yet, there is merit in keeping any unclearness or ambiguity that may affect the archaeological findings apart from any unclearness that may affect the reasoning about them.

So let us return to the reasoning and focus our attention once again on the second option described above, in which the findings are affirmative. That is, suppose that they include, in as unambiguous a way as possible, a large communal dining hall, a number of public baths, a pottery assemblage strictly unadorned, and so on. We are to imagine, then, an idealized, best-case, affirming scenario: the findings are all indeed clear-cut, and they are all positively correlated and maximally compatible with the Essene–center hypothesis. We have just noted, however, that the Essene–center hypothesis does not logically follow from these findings. What, then, are we to make of these findings?

---

9   There is a relationship between how surprising or improbable a piece of evidence is, given background assumptions, and its power to lend support to, or to confirm, a hypothesis. Put differently, confirmation is correlated with how much more probable the *evidence* is if the hypothesis is true than if the hypothesis is false. (See n. 12 below.) For more see Howson and Urbach, 1989, pp. 86–88. Also, for the notion of *strengthening* a hypothesis, see Scheffler, 1964, pp. 277ff.; and for Popper's notion of *corroborating* a hypothesis see Popper, 1959, appendix ix.

Background Expectations

Before abandoning the deductive approach in favor of a probabilistic one, let us turn our attention to the background assumptions and baseline expectations that operate here. The basic intuition seems to be that the more surprising and extraordinary are the affirming findings at Qumran, the more will it be in their power to help confirm the Essene-center hypothesis.[10] After all, an archaeological site of the Hasmonean–Herodian period is as a matter of routine expected to conform to one or another of a certain number of patterns familiar to the archaeologists of the period. These include, for example, military outposts, palaces, urban residences, villas, and port installations.[11] So if a site of that period conforms to none of the known patterns and yields surprising findings, it surely calls for an out-of-the-ordinary interpretation. If the features of the site of Qumran are indeed unique our confidence in the Essene–center hypothesis must surely be given a considerable boost. All the more so if these features are not only exceptional but also compatible with what were predicted as plausible material traces of an Essene community.

This seems to suggest that there was something not quite right in the idea of the simple "if-then" implication, as so far presented. Still within the framework of deductive reasoning, let us now consider a *double* implication instead, namely one that takes the form of an "if-and-only-if" statement. This statement asserts that there was an Essene center at Qumran *if, and only if*, the excavations at the site of Qumran turn up traces such as a large communal dining hall, or a number of ritual baths, or unadorned pottery, etc.

---

10 A consequence of the Bayesian approach to scientific reasoning is that "information that is particularly unexpected or surprising, unless some hypothesis is true, supports that hypothesis with particular force" (Howson and Urbach, 1989, p. 86). See also n. 12 below and its accompanying text.

11 Among the military outposts are Machaerus, Masada, and Herodium. Urban residences of the Herodian period were excavated in the Jewish Quarter in Jerusalem. Agricultural villas are mostly by springs, like Ein ez-Zara (the ancient Callirrhoe), Ein Feshkha, and En Boqeq (as well as the Ramat Hanadiv site in the north). Palaces are the royal Hasmonean and Herodian ones at Masada, Herodium, and Jericho. Relevant port installations are at Khirbet Mazin and Rujm el-Bahr.

What this double implication means is the following. To begin with, the archaeologists should determine what *distinctive* material traces, if any, an Essene settlement – and only an Essene settlement – would be likely to leave behind. Next, the archaeologists should proceed to look for these traces in their excavation of the site of Qumran. If the findings turn out (unambiguously) negative, this would refute the hypothesis about an Essene center at Qumran. But if they are (unambiguously) positive, the archaeologists *are* warranted in claiming an Essene character to the site of Qumran. The strength of the warrant will depend on the degree to which the archaeologists agree that the traces in question can best (and perhaps *only*) be explained if the site served as an Essene center.

The difference that the double implication makes is crucial, therefore. It makes it possible for the claim about an Essene settlement at Qumran to follow from the positive, affirming findings such as a dining hall or public baths, etc. No sleight of hand is involved here. The substance behind it is that in order to be able to assert the double implication the archaeologists have to be satisfied that they have indeed arrived at a list of items that only an Essene community could leave behind. The Essene hypothesis follows from the material findings only if these findings are *distinctive*, that is, if they are not consistent with any alternative theory, or explicable in any way other than the existence of an Essene center at the site of Qumran.

Prior Probabilities, Posterior Probabilities, and Interpretation

Both the implication ("if-then") sentence and the double implication ("if-and-only-if") sentence may help us get a clearer picture of our intuitive understanding of the problems involved. But they are too crude to model scientific reasoning (any scientific reasoning, not just in archaeology). Scientific practice is mostly probabilistic, not deductive.

There is in the philosophy of science a standard approach, referred to as Bayesian, which gives a systematic probabilistic account of the normative relationship between a theory and evidence adduced in its support. More specifically, it accounts for the degree to which we judge a theory, or hypothesis, probable, given particular evidence relating to it. It also accounts for the ways in which we change or update our judgment, in light of new evidence.

The key distinction here is between the *prior* probability of the theory and its *posterior* probability. The prior probability of a hypothesis H, or p(H), measures our belief in the hypothesis when we do not know the evidence E, and the posterior probability p(H|E) is the corresponding measure when we do. Coming to know E thus makes us update your probability assignment. It may help confirm the hypothesis – in which case p(H|E) is larger than p(H), disconfirm it – in which case p(H|E) is smaller than p(H), or leave it intact – in which case we say that E is irrelevant or neutral with respect to H. Any introduction of relevant new evidence will obviously change, upwards or downwards, the last measure we had. When new evidence E1 is introduced we may think of our latest measure of posterior probability p(H|E) as the new prior and repeat the procedure of updating: "Today's posterior distribution is tomorrow's prior" (Howson and Urbach, 1989, p. 80). Note that since the probability measures within this approach are subjective, or personal, you and I may differ in the prior probability we assign to H.

The formula that connects the posterior probability of a hypothesis H relative to evidence E with the prior probability of H is known as Bayes' theorem. It shows the posterior probability to be a function of the prior probability. I shall explain the formula not in the abstract but as already applied, or "translated" to the case in hand, by taking H to stand for the hypothesis that Qumran was an Essene center, namely the Qumran–Essene hypothesis, and E to stand for any piece of evidence considered to support the Qumran–Essene hypothesis – say, the finding of a scriptorium. What the formula in effect says is this: my posterior, updated probability that the Qumran–Essene hypothesis is true, given that I know a scriptorium was found at the site of Qumran, is equal to the prior probability measure I assigned to the Qumran–Essene hypothesis (before the scriptorium was excavated) multiplied by a certain factor. The multiplying factor is a fraction: its numerator is my assessment of the probability that a scriptorium will be found, conditional upon the truth of the Qumran–Essene hypothesis; its denominator is the prior probability I assign to the finding of a scriptorium at Qumran independently of the Qumran–Essene hypothesis.[12]

12   The formula is this:

The Bayesian model is normative. It sets an ideal for treating the complex relationship between theory and evidence. Outside of domains such as statistics and probabilistic reasoning, however, this standard is not always the regulative idea and in any case is not easily met. The archaeologists of Qumran did not operate within the Bayesian framework, and in this they were likely not exceptional. I shall later sketch an alternative approach (referred to as "presumptive") which I believe comes closer to describing how these scholars were actually operating. But the point of presenting the Bayesian approach at this stage is to highlight an important intuition that underlies it.

The intuition that the Bayesian model is designed to reflect is that accumulation of evidence ought to lead rational people to a converging posterior probability assessment, even if they start out from very different prior assessments. Rational people may indeed start out with widely different assessments of how probable some hypothesis (or future event) is. The point about rationality is that it has little to do with what our initial position is and everything to do with the way we revise and update our prior in light of new evidence. In the long run, if rational people agree on the evidence and if they abide by the Bayesian formula for the updating of their assessments, they will sooner or later converge on quite similar posterior assignments of probabilities.

But it seems that in the case of the Qumran–Essene hypothesis this does not happen. More than five decades after the initial excavation of

---

$$p(H|E) = p(H) \times p(E|H)/p(E)$$

The numerator of the fraction on the right-hand side of the formula is sometimes referred to as the *likelihood* of the evidence E on the hypothesis H, which is the converse of the degree of confirmation of hypotheses H, given evidence E. (The concept of likelihood is due to R. A. Fisher.) The denominator of the fraction in effect tells us how surprising (or unsurprising) is the particular piece of evidence E. And so, the fraction taken as a whole is in fact a measure of the distinctiveness of the evidence to the hypothesis. The extent to which evidence E confirms a hypothesis H increases with $p(E|H)$, while the power of E to confirm H depends on $p(E)$, i.e., on the probability of E when it is not assumed that H is true. In other words, the more surprising the evidence the greater it has confirming power. For more, see Howson and Urbach, 1989, part I; Hacking, 1965, chapter V.

the site, the controversy about the nature of the site does not diminish. What conclusion can we draw from this? Are we to conclude that there is a failure of rationality here, and that at least some of the protagonists in this controversy are irrational?

Well, irrationality is a possibility that cannot be ruled out. Indeed, many in the mainstream camp will be happy to adopt this conclusion (if they have not already done so). But I do not think that this is the only possibility. For one thing, the persistent divergence in the scholars' degree of belief in the Qumran–Essene hypothesis may simply indicate that these scholars do not operate within the Bayesian approach. I shall have more to say about what I take to be their approach later, but for now I want to point to an alternative possibility for explaining the persistent divergence whose implications are, I believe, deep.

The key is the condition mentioned above, that convergence on the posterior probability would occur in the long run provided that people "agree on the evidence." In the case of Qumran, however, this condition is not met. The protagonists in the controversy, while in some superficial sense equally "exposed" to all the relevant archaeological finds and data, do not agree on the evidence. It is not the case that everyone agrees that locus 30 is a scriptorium, or that the number of ritual baths (*Miqva'ot*) found at Qumran is exceptional, or that the cylindrical jars are unique, or that the animal bones are deliberate deposits, and so on. The assessment of each item of evidence depends on its description, and the description depends on its interpretation, and the interpretation in turn depends on the hypothesis one starts out with, which means, in effect, that it depends on the prior probability one assigns to the very Qumran–Essene hypothesis we set out to test. (More on description dependence in pp. 98–102 below.)

In other words, the issue of agreeing on the evidence is not independent of the issue of assigning prior probabilities to the hypothesis under consideration. Evidence and initial hypothesis are interdependent. And so the "probability kinematics" envisioned by the Bayesians (Jeffrey, 1983, pp. 164–175), with its convergent process of revising and updating, is aborted. Anyone who initially thought that the Qumran–Essene hypothesis is absurd, or highly unlikely, will dispute the very description of any piece of evidence that adherents of the hypothesis adduce in its support, let alone see it as increasing the probability of the hypothesis. And anyone who initially assigned a high probability to the hypothesis will interpret the findings and describe them in such a way that they will corroborate it.

I have maintained beforehand that widely different assignments of prior probability to a given hypothesis need not be incompatible with rationality or indicative of irrationality. I now want to draw a conclusion from the above discussion which I conjecture applies generally to the human sciences. It says that widely different assignments of prior probability to a given hypothesis are in and of themselves indicative of deep disagreements about the evidence. That is, people who start out with very different assessments of whether a given theory is probable will generally be unable to agree about the description and interpretation of almost any piece of evidence that is brought forth in support of the theory. The human sciences, understood to be dealing in an essential way with the interpretation of artifacts as products of human intentions, can thus be seen as ultimately concerned not with rationality or irrationality but with hermeneutics: in the final analysis the deep disagreements within these sciences are about meaning and interpretation.

THE TASK

A Two-Way Split

Let me backtrack now, to consider a more realistic account of the approach adopted by the archaeologists of Qumran. The excavation of Qumran, as we have seen, was not undertaken as a blind groping about. Rather, it was a motivated effort to test a specific hypothesis: namely, that the site of Qumran was an Essene center and that consequently it was connected to the scrolls.

Let us imagine that as the excavation proceeds the excavators become progressively convinced that, at least prima facie, the findings on the whole confirm rather than disconfirm the Qumran–Essene hypothesis. The excavators' efforts as of this point must divide in two directions. First, they must squarely face any negating finding and attempt to explain it away. Any finding that is, or appears to be, inconsistent with the Qumran–Essene hypothesis deserves special attention. Second, they must focus on the affirming findings. Here the task is to ascertain to what extent these findings are distinctive of an Essene settlement. With regard to each item they must not only raise the question whether it is consistent with the Qumran–Essene hypothesis, but also whether or not it is inconsistent with any of the other hypotheses that might be regarded as plausible alternatives to it. Let us consider some examples to illustrate both tasks.

Examples

Negating Findings

One set of findings at Qumran that was considered by some scholars to be problematic for the Qumran–Essene hypothesis consisted of the fortified tower and several additional items that were seen as traces of a battle that was apparently fought around the tower. These traces include Roman-type iron arrowheads and a layer of ash attesting to the burning of the roofs. Roland de Vaux, who excavated the site, concluded from these traces that the buildings were "reduced to ruins by military action" during the Jewish War of 68–73 (de Vaux, 1973, p. 36).

There are those who take these findings to contradict a much-cited description of the Essenes as peace loving people who "abhor all instruments of war."[13] Indeed at least one scholar takes the tower and the arrowheads as a cornerstone in his efforts to challenge the Qumran–Essene hypothesis.[14] The retort to this might be that the inhabitants of Qumran, although on the

---

13 Philo Judaeus, *Every Good Man is Free*, 78. However, Josephus speaks (a) of an Essene general; (b) of the Essenes habitually arming themselves against brigands when traveling (*War* 2 VIII 4:125). (See also Yadin, 1992a, p.178) It is also worth noting that the *War Scroll* portrays the Essenes as living in anticipation of a final and very real apocalyptic war. It is with these sources in mind that Magness remarks that "the question whether male sectarians engaged in combat or used weapons depends on the interpretation of the literary sources" (2002, p. 184).

14 Golb maintains (1995, *passim*) that the Qumran settlement was constructed as a fort in the Hasmonean period and continued to function as such throughout. Note that independently of the Qumran controversy, M. Har-El includes Qumran among what he refers to as a "ring of fortifications" surrounding Jerusalem, in his map in *Biblical Archaeologist* 1981.

whole peace loving, may well have fought the Romans in desperation on this particular occasion, when the Romans overran their settlement. The existence of a tower may attest to the fact that the inhabitants of Qumran were resolved to defend themselves rather than as evidence that the site was a fortress.

The second example concerns another potential embarrassment to the Essene–center hypothesis. It is the finding of the remains of several women and children among the excavated graves from the Qumran cemetery. This finding cries out for an explanation if the hypothesis about an all-male, celibate Essene community at Qumran is to be saved.[15]

15　The cemetery evidence is highly complex. De Vaux excavated 43 graves in the early 1950s and Steckoll ten more in 1966–1967. The whereabouts of only one of Steckoll's skeletons are currently known. Thirty nine of the skeletons excavated by de Vaux have recently been re-examined in Munich, Paris, and Jerusalem, using modern anthropological techniques. Of these, some 14–16 were found to be female and 5 were children: owing to the fragmentary state of the remains it is not always possible to determine the gender with certainty. Note that the examined skeletons represent less than four percent of the entire cemetery, which contains 1100–1200 graves (see n. 27 below). This sample, even if random, is too small on which to base any firm extrapolations. Still, it does suggest that the community at Qumran was predominantly male and that it is not likely to have included families. In addition, most of the female and children skeletons were found in what de Vaux referred to as the small "subsidiary cemeteries" to the north and south, while only two or three female skeletons were identified with a high degree of probability in the west-sector main cemetery. "This may indicate," says de Vaux in an attempt to explain away the embarrassment of female presence, "that the women were not members of the community, or at any rate not in the same sense as the men buried in the main cemetery. It may also signify that a development had taken place in the discipline of the community. The rule of celibacy may have been relaxed.... This would explain why the tombs of women are located in what seem to be extensions to the main cemetery" (1973, p. 129). In a more recent development, Zias (2000) argues that all the skeletons of women and children found in the subsidiary cemeteries are relatively recent Bedouin burials. This view has acquired significant, even if not universal, following: see, e.g., Magness, 2002, p. 172; Eshel et al., 2002, pp. 7, 18 (n. 59 and accompanying text). For disagreement, see Zangenberg, 2000, p. 6; Hirschfeld, 2003b, p. 39. For the latest view see Norton, 2003.

Clearly, invaluable information about the Qumran community could be gained had proper anthropological and medical studies been performed on all the skeletal remains in the entire cemetery. This, however, did not take place prior to 1967, when the site of Qumran was still in Jordanian hands, and there is no chance that it will be allowed under the auspices of the Israelis, for religious and religion-related political reasons.

Over the years scholars have argued in various ways that this finding is not inconsistent with the Qumran–Essene hypothesis. It was suggested, for example, that even though the inhabitants of the settlement at Qumran were celibate, some of them might have adopted celibacy only later in life. These sectarians could have had families before joining the Qumran community, and it is possible that their wives and children lived in the margins of the settlement or were in any case brought for burial there after their deaths. Whatever the explanations and whatever their degree of plausibility, however, in the last few years some scholars seem to converge on the view that almost all the skeletal remains of women and children in Qumran are later burials, perhaps even relatively recent Bedouin burials (see note 15). If this is indeed the case then the allegedly embarrassing negative finding is neatly explained away. Note that in this case the burden of proof shifts dramatically: the onus of providing an explanation for the virtually all-male cemetery now lies squarely on those who propose alternative theories to the Qumran–Essene hypothesis. (I shall return to discuss other aspects of the cemetery in pp. 99–102 below. Further negative findings, such as the so-called gendered objects or items potentially indicative of wealth, will also be discussed later.)

Affirming Findings: Ritual Baths

Turning to the task of assessing the probative value of the positive findings, I shall begin by considering the elaborate water-storage installations. Some scholars regard these installations as the dominant and most striking set of findings at Qumran. They include, in the first place, numerous cisterns and water channels. In addition, there are pools that seem to fit the traditional Jewish requirements for ritual bathing facilities, called *miqva'ot* (*miqveh*, in the singular).[16] The requirements in question stipulate the minimum

---

16 Here is a brief overview of the water system at Qumran, referred to by de Vaux as the most striking feature of the compound. The water system is organized along an elaborate and lengthy (approximately seven hundred meters long) aqueduct. This channel reaches into the hills behind Qumran to catch the torrential waterfalls down the cliffs at the head of Wadi Qumran and winds through the entire site, supplying all of its pools, from northwest to southeast, by means of branches of plaster-coated channels. Along its way there is one deep, round cistern (possibly from the Israelite

The archaeological site of Qumran. In the middle, stairs leading to a *miqveh* (ritual bath)
© The Israel Museum, Jerusalem / by Avraham Hai

volume of undrawn water (i.e., rain or spring water) a ritual bath must contain, and also that it must be dug into the ground without drains. As from the first century BCE an additional criterion that distinguishes a *miqveh* from a water-storage cistern is that the *miqveh* has steps, sometimes partitioned and sometimes not, leading into it. Given the intense concern of the Essenes with purification, as evidenced for example in the *Rule of the Community*,[17] this finding was hailed, from the early stages of the excavation, as confirming evidence for the Qumran–Essene hypothesis.

In order for the finding of the water installations to confirm the Qumran–Essene hypothesis at least two points have to be initially established. First, that these pools, or some of them, are indeed *miqva'ot*. Second, it has to be shown that the pools are not only consistent with the hypothesis but also distinctive to it.

The first requirement has to do with the problem of whether or not consensus can be reached regarding the interpretation of an archaeological finding. As it turns out no general consensus exists among the researchers about the definite identification of each and every Qumran pool as a ritual bath. De Vaux was careful in singling out as possible *miqva'ot* just two particular basins, which were "smaller and more carefully designed." He says: "They were certainly baths, but archaeology is powerless to determine whether the baths taken in them had a ritual significance" (1973, p. 132). However, much progress was made in the field of research of ancient *miqva'ot* in Palestine since de Vaux's time. "The evidence now

---

period, Iron Age II, 8th–6th century BCE; Hirschfeld dates it to the Hasmonean period) that was retained and refurbished by later inhabitants. The bulk of the water system is dated to the Hasmonean and Herodian periods, i.e., roughly to the two centuries before the destruction of the Jerusalem Temple (and of Qumran). The system includes a large number of additional cisterns, pools, and settling tanks ("decantation basins") of various sizes: depending on how one counts a few double-pools, and allowing for some differences between the main periods of occupation of the site, the total number is roughly 15–16. Some of the pools are stepped and plastered, and some have partitions running down the steps. Noted in their absence are bathhouses: there are no heated pools, mosaic floors, or built-up bathtubs at Qumran. (For more see Magness, 2002, pp. 54–55, 134–158; Hirschfeld believes that locus 34 is a built-up bathtub.)

17   1QS 3.4–9; 4.21; 5.13–14. Also in 11QT (the *Temple Scroll*) 49–51, CD (the *Damascus Document*) 10.11–14, in 4Q284, line 5, and more.

available," says Magness, "indicates that many of the pools at Qumran were used as *miqva'ot*, reflecting a concern with purity on the part of the site's inhabitants" (2002, p. 134). Hirschfeld counts seven (2003b, p. 30), while Reich, who is considered the leading expert among archaeologists on ritual baths in Judaea in the Second Temple period, identifies ten ritual baths in Qumran (1998, pp. 125–128). So we may safely take the first point as established and focus on the issue of distinctiveness.

It should be noted that there is some ambiguity about the requirement of distinctiveness in this context. That is, it is not altogether clear what precisely is being asked when we ask how distinctive to the Essene hypothesis the finding of ritual baths at Qumran is. Is it the very fact that ritual baths were found at Qumran that is supposed to be distinctive to the hypothesis? In other words, is it the case that *miqva'ot* are expected to be found at the site of Qumran if, and only if, the site was an Essene settlement? Or, alternatively, is it only the finding of an unusually large number of ritual baths that is supposed to be distinctive to the hypothesis? If the latter, then some indication is needed as to what would be the normal expectation.

It has often been pointed out that most of the alternative interpretations of the site of Qumran – whether military outpost, official customs post, agricultural manor house, or industrial plant – see it as a Jewish site. As such, it would reasonably be expected to comprise facilities for ritual bathing. After all, the commandment of ritual bathing applies to all Jews, not just to Essenes. Moreover, since Qumran is a hot and arid desert site, with a short and intense season of torrential rains, it would be expected to comprise a well-developed system of water reservoirs which would make the site inhabitable all year round. So we need to know with a reasonable degree of confidence how many of the water pools at Qumran were designed for ritual bathing purposes rather than for general practical purposes. Until there is consensus among the researchers regarding this pivotal question it must remain inconclusive whether or not the number of *miqva'ot* at Qumran exceeds normal expectations and is indeed unusually large.[18]

---

18 Hirschfeld addresses this point and concludes as follows: "At the time of the excavation of Qumran, in de Vaux's days, the number of *miqva'ot* at Qumran was considered

Affirming Findings: Scriptorium

The second example of a positive finding concerns the so-called scriptorium. Here is how de Vaux presents us with this crucial finding, "the long room which extends southwards from the tower":

> The room was filled with the debris from the upper floor – which had fallen in at the end of Period II. In this debris were found fragments of structures made of mud-brick covered with carefully smoothed plaster. These mysterious fragments were collected and taken to Jerusalem where they were painstakingly re-assembled. In this way it was found possible to reconstruct a table from them a little more than 5 m. in length, 40 cm. in breadth, and only 50 cm. in height. There were also fragments from two smaller tables.... This might have suggested the furniture of a dining-room except for the fact that we had already identified this in another part of the buildings which did not contain a table.... Furthermore two inkwells were found among the debris...of a type known...to belong to the Roman Period (1973, pp. 29–30)

At issue, then, is a long, second-floor room known as loc. 30 whose distinctive features include an elongated, narrow, mud-brick low table, two additional smaller tables, the remains of a low, mud-brick bench attached to the wall, and two inkwells.[19] Some researchers point out that the furniture

---

exceptional. But today, after much research and many more excavations have been conducted in Second-Temple sites, the number of *miqva'ot* at Qumran, while admittedly large, is not exceptional.... It is close to the norm governing rich Jewish homes in the Second-Temple period" (2003b, pp 30–31, my translation). This claim is contested by Broshi (2003, p. 67); Broshi also believes that the fact that Qumran comprises the second largest *miqveh* out of about 600 *miqva'ot* found in Palestine carries significant weight. Magness reports a particular set of calculations (by Bryant Wood) according to which "the pools at Qumran contained an excessive amount of water even for a community of 200 living in the desert, and therefore some of them must have been used as *miqva'ot*" (2002, p. 147). She also reports that Reich has demonstrated that "the amount of space occupied by the pools in relation to the total size of the settlement at Qumran is proportionate to that occupied by *miqva'ot* in contemporary villas in Jerusalem's Jewish quarter" (p. 153).

19 One inkwell is of pottery and the other of bronze. Another inkwell was found in the adjacent room (locus 31): see Magness, 2002, p. 60. It is fair to note that inkwells are

may suggest a dining room – a "triclinium" where diners reclined on the benches. Others maintain that the bench is too narrow to serve the purpose of sitting on it, let alone reclining on it (Reich, 1995). Note however that de Vaux summarily rejects the dining-room interpretation for what we may take to be an external rather than an internal reason, namely, that another locus at the site (loc. 77) had already been identified as a dining room. It is at this point that de Vaux presents his own interpretation. Strikingly, it is phrased as a question:

> Is it not reasonable to regard these tables and inkwells as the furniture of a room where writing was carried on, a *scriptorium* in the sense in which this term later came to be applied to similar rooms in monasteries of the Middle Ages? (p. 30).

There can be little doubt that it was this scriptorium hypothesis which, in conjunction with the scrolls themselves, ignited the imagination of the world. The medieval, monastic connotations of this term were sufficient to portray Qumran as the first monastery in the Western world, with the Essenes as the first monks. (Contrary to a widespread belief, de Vaux himself never explicitly describes the site as such; see Chapter One, n. 22.) Needless to say, it was this interpretation that came under the hottest fire in the following years. It was pointed out, for example, that scribes at that time were known to have been writing on their laps while sitting on the floor, rather than writing at a table while seated on a bench.

Had consensus existed among scholars that this particular upper-floor room is indeed to be identified as a scriptorium, this would have been highly significant. The finding of a scriptorium at Qumran would not merely have been consistent with the hypothesis that the scrolls were of Essene provenance and were written at Qumran, but it would have been highly distinctive to it. In terms of the double-implication ("if-and-only-if") formula discussed earlier, this means that we would be in a position to assert both of its components. Namely: *if* Qumran functioned as an

---

rare finds in archeological sites in the Land of Israel. It is therefore not surprising to find them featuring on so many covers of so many books about the Dead Sea scrolls and Qumran.

Essene site, *then* the excavation of the site would yield a space fit to serve as a scriptorium – and *only if* Qumran functioned as an Essene site, would the excavation of the site yield a space fit to serve as a scriptorium. Only in a site occupied by a community devoted to copying and possibly to composing manuscripts would the finding of a scriptorium be expected and accounted for.

The finding of a scriptorium is therefore different from the case of the ritual baths discussed above. With regard to the ritual baths, as we saw, the crux of the problem is not in the identification of the cisterns, or at least of some of them, as *miqva'ot*; rather, it is in figuring out how distinctive to the Essene hypothesis such a finding is. More specifically, and trickier still, the problem consists in achieving sufficient clarity about background expectations: just how many *miqva'ot* would be distinctive to the Essene hypothesis? In the case of the scriptorium, on the other hand, there can be no question as to the distinctiveness of such a finding to the Essene hypothesis. A scriptorium is consistent with the hypothesis maintaining the threefold connection among Qumran, Essenes, and the scrolls – and only with this hypothesis. The serious problem here pertains to the very interpretation of the finding as a room designed and designated for scribal activity.

Affirming Findings: The Yahad *Ostracon*
A more recently unearthed finding is hailed by some as providing the most clinching piece of affirming evidence to date for the Qumran–Essene hypothesis; to others this finding, while interesting in itself, is indifferent as far as the hypothesis is concerned.

In a 1996 excavation at the site of Qumran conducted by James F. Strange from the University of South Florida, Tampa, a first century ostracon (fragment of pottery used as a writing tablet) was discovered. Written in Hebrew, this ostracon is the only writing found at Qumran since the discovery of the scrolls in the nearby caves nearly fifty years earlier. Scholars are sharply divided, however, as to the proper deciphering of the ostracon, which is broken into two fragments: a single word at the critical point where the ostracon breaks is at the center of the controversy.

Two readings of the ostracon have been offered, both by prominent scholars and experts in Hebrew paleography. The first reading is offered by the veteran scrolls scholar Frank Moore Cross of Harvard University and Esther Eshel of the Hebrew University, the second by the renowned Hebrew palaeographer Ada Yardeni. While widely different in their implications, both readings share a rendering of the ostracon as a transfer of property. Both seem to agree that the ostracon tells us that in "the second year" a transfer of (among other things) some fig trees took place in Jericho to a person named Elazar. At issue is a three-letter word (or four letters, inclusive of the preposition "to") that Cross and Eshel read as *yahad* (Cross and Eshel, 1997a). Significantly, the word *yahad* is the epithet that occurs in reference to the scrolls community, most notably in the *Rule of the Community*. If the reading of Cross and Eshel is right and the ostracon indeed records a gift of property to the *yahad*, then the discovery of the ostracon would seem to confirm that the site of Qumran, where it was found, served as a center of the community. Moreover, the ostracon can then indeed be seen as the "first find from Khirbet Qumran that provides proof of the link between the site and the scrolls" (Cross and Eshel, 1997b, p. 40). Yardeni, however, reads the crucial word differently. Seeing the word as comprised of three letters (without the prepositional 'l'), she reads it as *aher*, meaning 'another'. Her rendering of the entire line is 'every other tree' (Yardeni, 1997).

The dispute is acute, with much at stake. It turns, in the last analysis, on issues such as whether the salient diagnostic feature that distinguishes the Hebrew *dalet* ('d') from *resh* ('r') in the first century formal and cursive scripts is or is not contained in the minuscule right shoulder of the letter which is barely legible at the breaking point of this ostracon. For every scholar who would love to see the word *yahad* in line eight of the ostracon's blurred, fading and badly broken up letters there are several other scholars who are frustrated by what they see as a case of wishful deciphering. In the end, the reading of the crucial word *yahad* in the ostracon would seem to remain highly tendentious, conferring a rather questionable degree of support to the considerable historical claim made for it.

Threshold Effects

As we have seen, the archaeologists must account for, or explain away, findings that are seemingly negative to their favorite hypothesis. They must also consider the contribution of each positive finding to the confirmation of the hypothesis from the point of view of its distinctiveness to that hypothesis. But this is not all. They must consider in addition what may be termed *threshold effects*. This relates to the question of whether the positive findings are to be taken jointly or severally.

Let us suppose that b_1, b_2, and b_3 are traces which, if found, are considered distinctive of an Essene settlement. For example, a large number of baths, a scriptorium, and a cemetery that comprises male skeletons only. What would it take for the threshold of confirmation to be attained? Is it required that the Essene hypothesis be confirmed by each of these items separately, or is it rather their combination that will do it? Must each of these items be "strong" enough to pass the threshold and confirm the hypothesis on its own, or are they allowed to form a cluster so that together they will confirm the hypothesis? In short, is the hypothesis supposed to be inferred from a *disjunction* of findings ("If b_1 *or* b_2 *or* b_3 are found, then Qumran was Essene"), or from a *conjunction* of findings ("If b_1 *and* b_2 *and* b_3 are found then Qumran was Essene")?

In the disjunctive case each of the items, if indeed found, is considered a sufficient condition for the confirmation of the hypothesis. This means that each item is striking, distinctive, and diagnostic. This occurs when there is a high degree of consensus among researchers about the identification and interpretation of each of these items. These are difficult standards to meet. In the conjunctive case an allowance is made for this difficulty: it is the whole cluster of findings that is the sufficient condition for the confirmation of the hypothesis, not each item on its own. Allowance is also made for the messiness and open-ended nature of archaeological findings. The emphasis here is on a *Gestalt* – a holistic picture that may be compelling even if none of its items is compelling in isolation. The price for this allowance, however, is that a larger number of confirming items is required. Each item is here thought of as a necessary component in a cluster that, taken as a whole, is a sufficient condition for the confirmation of the hypothesis.[20]

---

20 This condition is sometimes referred to as NESS, or "Necessary Element of a Sufficient Set." Note that the discussion in this section is within an intuitive, deductive framework, rather than a probabilistic-Bayesian one.

ASSESSMENT

Test or Presumption?

In setting out to test a hypothesis, the probative value of each piece of evidence that comes to light has to be assessed. The question asked is whether the new finding raises or lowers the probability that the hypothesis under consideration is true, given the previous pieces of evidence. Ideally, the investigator should be able to attach numerical values to these assessments. The updated assessment, given the entire body of evidence, indicates the degree to which the hypothesis is confirmed or disconfirmed.

This is the gist of the Bayesian approach (outlined above, in pp. 74–78). It is a confirmation oriented, normative approach whose main emphasis is on the dynamics of revising one's degree of belief in the hypothesis under consideration with the addition of new evidence. A rival, non-Bayesian normative approach is the Popperian one, whose orientation is on refutation. It encourages the investigator to come up with the most daring – and hence sometimes initially least probable – hypothesis and to subject it to a series of crux experiments. The experiments are meant to test the hypothesis by attempting to refute it. So long as it survives such tests, it is retained.

In the case of Qumran it is quite clear that the archaeologists adhered to neither of the two normative approaches. I want now to try to reconstruct the logic that I believe underlies the approach actually adopted by the practitioners. As it turns out, the practitioners' method combines elements from both of the normative models.

Their starting point accords with the confirmation oriented approach. They started with the Qumran–Essene hypothesis, which to them was most sensible and to which they assigned a high prior probability, given their background knowledge from the scrolls and the contemporary first century literary sources. But they can hardly be described as having proceeded with the incremental updating process envisaged by the Bayesian model. It would be more accurate to describe them as starting out with a *presumption in favor* of this hypothesis. A presumption in favor of a hypothesis means, essentially, that the hypothesis is taken to be true, unless and until it is refuted.[21] From this point on, the focus is on potential refutation. Each

---

21 For a theory of presumption see Ullmann-Margalit, 1983.

piece of potentially refuting evidence is regarded as a crux experiment, taken one at a time without letting such pieces of evidence accumulate. If the hypothesis withstands several crux experiments of this sort, namely, if the potentially damaging pieces of evidence are successfully explained away, then the theory is accepted as true. It becomes the consensus and scholars who resist it are met with suspicion and hostility.

To elucidate the presumptive approach further, we can imagine a scale on which we assign each item ("finding") either to the positive side (a confirming piece of evidence) or to the negative side (a disconfirming piece of evidence). A neutral possibility also exists in which an item belongs on neither side of the scale since it neither confirms nor disconfirms the hypothesis. The idea is that at the end we should be able to read off the scales which side, if any, outweighs the other, and thus reach a conclusion as to whether the hypothesis is confirmed or disconfirmed. If we start out with a presumption in favor of a hypothesis, this will mean that from the outset the scale will not be empty and equally balanced. Rather, one side of the scale will be loaded from the start: some initial weight will be placed on the positive side to reflect the presumption that the hypothesis is true *unless* refuted.

The procedure of weighing, within the presumptive approach, is such that we focus chiefly on potentially refuting items. No special attention is therefore given to the difference between confirming items that are distinctive to the hypothesis under consideration, and neutral items that are merely consistent with the hypothesis but may be consistent with alternative hypotheses just as well. Questions relating to threshold effects tend to be disregarded as well. As a result, all non-negative items will pile up indiscriminately on the confirming side of the scale. But we treat differently the negative items, which have the potential to refute the hypothesis. Each seemingly negative item is put separately on the negative side of the scale to see whether or not it succeeds in outweighing the positive side. If we judge that it does not, we discard it altogether and turn to repeat the procedure with the next negative item. That is, the negative items are assessed individually and are not allowed to pile up. (They are not part of a revising or "updating" process as envisaged by the Bayesian model.)

This means that the onus of rebutting the presumption in favor of the hypothesis is put on each negative item individually, and a very onerous burden it is. In the case of the Qumran–Essene hypothesis in hand the focus is on each purportedly negative item such as the fortified tower, the female skeletons, the so-called gendered objects, the items potentially indicative of wealth, or what have you. Each such item is carefully considered and weighed, and so long as it is taken by general consensus not to refute the hypothesis conclusively, the presumption holds and the hypothesis is retained.

On my reconstruction, then, the archaeologists' attitude toward the Qumran–Essene hypothesis can be more accurately captured by saying that they presumed it to be true than by maintaining that they were seeking to test whether or not it was true. I leave open the question of assessing how good – or how typical in the various sciences – is this presumptive approach. My intuitive judgment is that it is superior to the refutationist method of Popper. As for its comparison with the Bayesian method I will point out, first, that few if any of the empirical branches of science do measure up to the Bayesian strictures, and second, that in comparison to the Bayesian approach the presumptive one is eminently intuitive and practical. In any case, this reconstruction helps explain, I believe, the considerable effort on the part of the adherents of the Qumran–Essene hypothesis to explain away any negative finding. It also helps us understand how it is that the important issue of the potential distinctiveness of some of the positive findings to the Qumran–Essene hypothesis remains somewhat out of focus and gets watered down by the mass of otherwise non-negative evidence.

Confirmation Bias

Let me at this point digress briefly to psychology. In addition to the presumptive attitude there is a mechanism that may help explain why the confirming side of the scale tends to seem more weighty and substantial than it really is. It is a mechanism well known to psychologists, who refer to it as *confirmation bias*.

A confirmation bias confers advantage on the hypothesis or belief that one holds over alternative or competing hypotheses, simply in virtue of the fact that it *is* the hypothesis or belief that one holds. In discussing this phenomenon, psychologist Joshua Klayman (1995) talks about what he calls "positive hypothesis testing." Ordinary people and researchers alike tend to look for and focus on features that are expected to be present if the hypothesis is true. Moreover, they are in general unaware of the fallacy discussed earlier, that the presence of such features, even in quantity, does not by itself conclusively verify the hypothesis.

As an example, suppose that you believe in astrology. Your hypothesis regarding Pisceans (born between February 20 and March 20) is that they are creatures entirely of instinct, highly imaginative and creative. Also, you believe them to be unreliable, easily influenced by others, and helplessly fond of drugs and alcohol. What you are likely to do, if you are a typical hypothesis holder, is to be generally on the lookout for people who conform to this profile, and to be impressed when, upon being asked, they tell you that they are indeed Pisces. This is fine, as long as you realize that however many such people you encounter, you will not have thereby confirmed your hypothesis.

What will in general not occur to you is to be on the lookout for disconfirming evidence, that is, to look for Pisces who do *not* conform to the Pisces profile. Thus, you might want to look for people who conform, say, to the following profile: "organized, fastidious and pedantic, law abiding, protocol following, and readers of small print" (a profile that any amateur astrologer will immediately recognize as Virgo) and to ask *them* what their zodiac is. You should be quite troubled if you find that some of these people are Pisces because in such a case your favorite hypothesis will be in trouble. But you are not likely to be confronted with such evidence, even if it exists. The conclusion is that people fall for the confirmation bias in that they exhibit "an inclination to retain, or a disinclination to abandon, a currently favored hypothesis" (Klayman, 1995, p. 386).[22]

Still, for the sake of fairness, it has to be pointed out that we often exhibit a confirmation bias in favor of a hypothesis that is in fact true. To show a confirmation bias at work in favor of some hypothesis is one thing, and to prove the hypothesis wrong is quite another.

---

22   For more on cognitive confirmation bias and related literature, see Ben-Shakhar et al., 1998.

FRAMING FINDS AS FACTS

Artifacts

Archaeology and geology share some important interests. Archaeologists and geologists alike dig into the ground; archaeologists and geologists alike are interested in stratigraphy. They seek to differentiate among historical (and pre-historical) layers, to date them, and to account for them. A crucial difference between the practitioners of geology and of archaeology is that while the former are concerned exclusively with the results of natural processes, the latter deal primarily with artifacts: archaeology thus belongs to the human sciences, geology does not. Artifacts are human products, intentionally made with a purpose in mind. To account for an artifact – a clay vessel, an iron nail, a stone ossuary, or whatever – involves more than an account of its structural properties. It is to account for it *qua* product of human agency. It involves an understanding of its function, of the intention behind its manufacture or use. A geologist might tell us about the composition, the origin, and the age of a certain piece of rock; the archaeologist will inform us that it is a boulder for marking a grave, or the base of a column. "Function is a critical aspect of most human artifacts," the psychological literature about perception tells us: "What an object is being used for has measurable effects on what people are likely to call it" (Miller and Johnson-Laird, 1976, p. 229).

Accounting for artifacts, therefore, is an essentially interpretative enterprise. Whether a firm horizontal surface protruding from the wall is a bench to sit (or recline) on, or a table for copying documents, or a shelf for storing documents and books surely has to do with its observable properties such as width, height, and firmness. But ultimately it remains a matter of interpretation. "The peculiar aspect of archaeology as a discipline is dictated by the peculiar nature of its data – observations about artifacts and their attributes" (Clarcke, 1968, p. 20). The attributes in question are not just, and even not primarily, the observable structural ones of the object in question: they are the intentional functional ones. And the "observations" about such attributes are anything but observations in the perceptual sense. They are observations in the sense of speculative interpretations – they speculate about the intention behind the object, they interpret its use.

In the course of discussing the nature of the archaeological argument thus far, some of the archaeological data of Qumran were discussed as well, serving an illustrative purpose. Mention was thus made of the fortified tower, the cisterns, the cemetery, and the scriptorium. At this point I should like to pay more direct and detailed attention to further archaeological findings from Qumran. The aim is not to survey these finds as such; rather, it is to highlight the interpretative problem of framing finds as facts.

The Case of the Bone Deposits

Take the case of bare animal bones that were found in multiple free spaces between the buildings in the compound of Qumran. Animal bones by themselves are just bones, not artifacts. But qua buried bones, or for that matter qua deposited bones, they involve human agency. The bones were arranged and deposited flush with the level of the ground in jars covered by lids, or between large pieces of pottery, or just covered by a plate but not covered with earth. The bones were taken apart and were clean of flesh at the time they were deposited. They belonged to sheep or goats, to lambs or kids, and to cows or oxen.

One may continue this description of the find by supplying more factual details about it: by citing the precise locations in the site where the deposits were found, or specifying the size, composition, and type of pottery relating to each single deposit, and so on. It is one thing, however, to enumerate every "neutral" fact about this find, and it is a very different thing to introduce this find the way de Vaux does.

De Vaux presents the find of the bones immediately after discussing the communal dining room. He links the two topics with the following statement: "Some, at least, of these meals [eaten in the dining-room] seem to have had a religious significance" (1973, p. 12). Moreover, the lengthy description that ensues of the various factual aspects of the bone deposits ends as follows: "The care with which the bones were set apart after the flesh had been cooked and eaten reveals a religious preoccupation.... These deposits do constitute clear evidence of the fact that certain of the meals eaten in the main chamber which we have described had a religious significance" (ibid., p. 14).

Whatever the deposits may or may not constitute, de Vaux's description constitutes a framing of the facts. Indeed, the case in hand well illustrates Clarcke's dictum: "The archaeologist's facts are artifacts – and their context" (1968, p. 14). As pointed out, while animal bones as such are not artifacts, their burial, in all its aspects, makes them artifacts. And the context in which these artifacts are presented by de Vaux is of a religious ritual. It is the context that is supposed to endow the material finding with significance, for it provides an interpretation, or at least hints at a possible direction where an interpretation may be sought; it attempts to answer a particular "why" question.

It is interesting to note that the bone deposits correspond to no known Jewish commandment, rite, or practice. The religious context suggested by de Vaux, and accepted by the consensus view, is thus only a promissory note, or a "place-holder" for an explanation: it is a hint as to what sort of an explanation is to be sought. De Vaux himself lists several speculations by different scholars concerning a possible explanation of the bone deposits (1973, pp. 14–16, n. 3). The free-floating scholarly imagination in this regard ranges from the arguable common sense to the colorful far-fetched. Here is a glimpse:

- The bones are the remains of sacrifices of firstborn of clean animals;
- The bones are the remains of sacrifices for the consecration of a sanctuary;
- The bones were regarded by the Qumran community as impure and were buried in pots or beneath shards in order to avoid their being inadvertently touched;
- The bones were buried because bones belonging to meat that has been consecrated by blessing cannot simply be thrown away but must be buried;
- The bones were not deliberately buried but rather "abandoned on the spot when a festal banquet was tragically interrupted by an enemy attack" (Laperrousaz, 1976);
- The bones attest to the fact that Qumran was a cultic center where sacrifices were made (Humbert, 2003a). It should be noted, however, that no altar or other facility suitable for ritual sacrifice has been excavated at Qumran;

- The bones "represent the remains of occasional sacral or ritual meals that were non-sacrificial" (Magness, 2002, p. 118);[23]
- The bones have "prosaic," non-religious explanations. They were used: (1) for improvement of the soil; or (2) as part of the perfume industry that was practiced at Qumran (Hirschfeld, 2003b, pp. 11, 34);[24] Hirschfeld rejects the description of the bones as "deposited."

Lawrence Schiffman (1994) offers a different framing of the finding of the bone deposits. His very brief mention of the find is presented in the context of adducing evidence that the community of Qumran was sizable. "We also can derive evidence of large–group occupation from the considerable number of bones of edible animals found buried between the buildings in pottery containers, a practice otherwise unknown in Jewish tradition" (p. 45). Schiffman relates to the bones, then, simply as remnants of meals. But he cannot of course ignore the entrenched religious framing of the find and in the very next sentence he goes on to deny the sacrifice hypothesis. He bases this denial not on archaeological evidence but rather, strikingly, on textual evidence gleaned from the scrolls. "It is important to stress that these bones could not have been the remains of sacrifices, because the literary evidence strongly indicates that ritual sacrifice at Qumran would have been unacceptable to the sectarians" (ibid.).

This is yet another example of the circular manner in which the writings and the ruins are occasionally used for purposes of mutual corroboration. (This topic was discussed at length in Chapter One, pp. 41–49.) The archaeological data are being surveyed for the insight they might offer for the interpretation of the scrolls, while at the same time the data themselves are being interpreted in light of the very same textual material from the scrolls. Schiffman does not even hint at the possibility that, to the extent

---

23 Magness' position deserves to be spelled out a bit further. She first explores the archaeological find of the bones from all its aspects, and then examines it in light of various ancient textual sources – literary, halakhic, and the scrolls. This examination leads her to the following conclusion. "It is more likely that just as the sectarians considered their communal meals to be a substitute for participation in the Temple cult, they treated the animals consumed at these meals in a manner analogous to the Temple sacrifices, although they were not technically sacrifices" (2002, p. 119).

24 Eshel dismisses this claim with sarcasm (2003, p. 58).

that the buried bones do suggest some sacrificial rite, this may be taken as evidence *undermining* the presumed link between the scrolls and the site of Qumran.

Yet another way to frame the finds of animal bones is offered by Lena Cansdale (1997). Her conjecture about Qumran is that it was a priestly establishment. She believes that it functioned as a customs post, and possibly as an inn as well, under the control of what she terms "the official Jericho priestly functionaries." Cansdale's discussion of the animal bone deposits is in the context of her general survey of food remains in Qumran. She is interested in finding out what these may tell us about the food production and food cultivation activities of the Qumran community.

What is notable to her about the bone finds is what they do *not* include. She points out that no fowl bones were found. In her mind, this absence raises a question since chickens are considered clean animals and ample evidence exits that from the Hellenistic period onwards fowl were raised and consumed. However, as she points out, there is a Mishnaic decree according to which priests were forbidden to raise chickens. Cansdale adduces this decree, along with the absence of chicken bones from the bone deposits at Qumran, in support of her hypothesis that Qumran was a priestly establishment.

Facts under Description

The puzzle raised by Cansdale about the absence of fowl bones among the finds of bones at Qumran may help highlight the nature of other puzzles concerning other finds. Suppose an artifact X is found in the course of an archaeological excavation, raising the question "how do we account for X." It is quite natural to interpret this, at least initially, as asking "why is X there," in other words, how do we account for the *presence* of X in the context in which it was found. However, the question about the presence of X can in principle be taken in two ways: it may ask how did X come to be there in the first place, or it can ask what the function of X was.[25]

For example, consider the finding at Qumran of a large assemblage of neatly stacked pottery. This assemblage was found in one particular room

25 For an elaboration see Ullmann-Margalit, 1978.

and it consisted of more than one thousand items, mostly undecorated plates, bowls, and cups. The natural questions to ask are: How are we to understand this pottery assemblage? What was its function? In contrast to what are we to evaluate it? Or, indeed, what was the function of the room in which it was found? The standard and generally accepted account, following de Vaux, is that this room (loc. 86, 89) was a storage room; more particularly, that it was used to store the dishes used for the communal sectarian meals eaten in the adjacent dining room, or "refectory" (loc. 77). As Magness puts it, "The inhabitants practiced a deliberate and selective policy of isolation, manufacturing ceramic products to suit their special needs and concerns with purity. It is clear that they chose to manufacture and use undecorated pottery instead of fine wares" (2002, p. 89). Cansdale's alternative account maintains that it was a kitchen inventory of an inn (1997). Further interpretations that were offered for the same find see it as a potter's storeroom, or possibly a shop (Donceel and Donceel-Voûte, 1994; Hirschfeld, 2003b, p. 28).[26]

But often further questions or puzzles are raised with regard to a particular aspect of a finding. Sometimes it is impossible to come to a shared and agreed-upon description of the finding. Any description of the item to be explained reflects prior assumptions and expectations on the part of the researcher, and frames the finding in a particular context (see pp. 77–78 above). Take, for example, the case of the Qumran cemetery. What is the question one wants to ask with regard to the findings of the cemetery? Suppose one's starting point is the consensual presumption that the Qumran community was Essene, and thus celibate. If so, then one's pressing concern about the cemetery is how to account for the skeletons of women and children found in it. The X to be accounted for is not just "a cemetery"; it is, rather, "a female-containing-cemetery." In contrast, if one starts from the assumption that Qumran was some sort of a conventional, non-monastic, community, one's question about the cemetery would have to be the opposite one, namely – how to account for the very small number of skeletons of women and children found there. So the X to be accounted for is now "a predominantly-male-cemetery."

---

26 Again, while only one or two researchers hold these alternative accounts, they serve the intended illustrative purpose. (See n. 5 above.)

Another puzzle about the cemetery involves the number of graves: almost twelve hundred were counted.[27] This is a large number, relative to any estimate about the size of the Qumran community.[28] The attempt to explain the large number of graves by suggesting that the community that occupied the site of Qumran had been using the cemetery over many generations may run into difficulties too. Some scholars point out that the graves at Qumran appear to be on the same horizontal level, and this fact is generally taken to suggest burial over a relatively short period of time.[29] Further questions have to do with other unusual aspects of the cemetery such as the regularity of the graves, the uniform style of stone overlay, the fact that they are individual rather than family graves,[30] the north–south orientation of most of the graves,[31] and more.[32]

---

27 The number of graves has until recently been in dispute. A study by Kapera (2000), based on air photography, estimates the number at 711. By Hirschfeld's count (2003b, p. 38), based on a land survey, the number of graves is 823. An extensive and highly detailed mapping of the cemetery, undertaken in 2001, is reported in Eshel et al., 2002. It says: "Our mapping of the cemetery allows us to ascertain that there were more than 1138 tombs in the cemetery east of Khirbet Qumran" (p. 144). The reliability of the land-penetrating radar technique that was used in this mapping is, however, questioned by some scholars.

28 "There is a manifest disproportion between the number of the tombs and the number of inhabitants for whom there was room in the buildings" (De Vaux, 1973, p. 56). On the size of the population at Qumran scholars' estimates differ markedly: Milik places it at 150–200 people (1959, p. 97); Broshi at 120–150 (2001a, pp. 209–210); Patrich at 50–70 (1994, pp. 93–94), subsequently revised to 30–50 (1998, p. 66); Humbert's estimate of 10–15 people is the lowest (1994, pp. 170–173).

29 All of these considerations are taken by Golb to support his view that the cemetery was a military cemetery for "the warriors who fought at Qumran"(1995, p. 34). But he does not address the vexing question of who might have done the burying of these many hundreds of fallen soldiers.

30 Jews living in Judaea in the first century BCE and the first century CE mostly used to "bury their dead in underground, rock-cut burial caves consisting of one or more rooms, which were used by extended families over the course of several generations" (Magness, 2002, p. 174).

31 According to Eshel et al., of the 1138 tombs at least 999 are north–south in orientation. "It seems likely that the fifty-four that are east–west in orientation are tombs of people buried in the cemetery over the last few centuries" (2002, p. 144).

32 However, at Ein el–Ghuweir, some seven kilometers south of Qumran, Bar-Adon discovered two small cemeteries (1977). He pronounced them to be identical in form

Yet another question about the cemetery, which frames it very differently, has to do with its distance from the building complex. Norman Golb cites in this context the Mishnaic ruling that requires, for reasons of ritual purity, a distance of at least fifty cubits between a Jewish settlement and an adjacent cemetery. According to Golb, the graves nearest the walls of the settlement at Qumran are thirty five meters away. Given that a cubit is roughly an arm's length (just about half a meter), Golb asserts that "this just barely satisfied" the requirement of the Mishnah. He then goes on to say: "It is impossible to believe, however, that the purity–obsessed brethren described in the *Manual of Discipline*, who were governed by priests, would have allowed themselves to build a communal cemetery so close to their settlement, particularly when more abundant space was available farther away" (1995, p. 34). He concludes in characteristic no uncertain terms: "The close proximity of the graves to the settlement by itself proves that the people who wrote the *Manual of Discipline* – or indeed any other such purity–brotherhood – could have had nothing whatever to do with Khirbet Qumran" (ibid.).[33]

Each of these puzzles and questions focuses on a different aspect of the item to be explained. And an item-to-be-explained (an *explanandum*) is always relative to a particular description. Therefore, it is not "the

---

with the tombs of the main cemetery at Qumran and held that they were Essene and related to the sectarian community at Qumran. Of the twenty graves he examined, seven were not of adult males: six women and one child. (An additional twenty-grave cemetery was found at Hiam el-Sagha, in the hills above Ein el-Ghuweir. This cemetery too was similar in construction, and in the unusual north–south orientation of the graves, to the cemeteries at Qumran and Ein el-Ghuweir.)

De Vaux warned that it is "rash" to suppose that Ein el-Ghuweir or the cemetery near it were Essene, and Magness concludes that although the settlement at Ein el-Ghuweir was contemporary with Qumran and was inhabited by Jews, the sum total of the archaeological evidence from there as well as from recent excavations at the Nabatean cemetery of Khirbet Quazone, indicate that "the type of cemetery found at Ein el-Ghuweir is not necessarily sectarian" (2002, p. 223).

33 S. H. Steckoll (1968) makes an opposite use of the very same figure of thirty-five meters. Accepting that Qumran was inhabited by purity-observant sectarians, he takes this to support the view that the Mishnaic ruling was already in force in the Second Temple period, precisely because the measured distance is *within* the critical distance of fifty cubits.

cemetery" as such which calls for explanation but rather a "close-to-the-settlement cemetery," or an "over-sized cemetery," or again a "regular and uniform cemetery." These descriptions, as we saw, are far from being "neutral." They frame the findings. They reflect what it is that the researcher finds surprising about them and in this sense they reveal the researcher's preconceptions. "Archaeological facts or data change in the changing light of what the archaeologist deems 'significant attributes' "(Clarcke, 1968, p. 15). Hence the elusiveness of archaeological "finds"; hence the essential softness of the "hard" material facts of archaeology. The non-convergence of opinions on the dominant Qumran–Essene theory is also a result of the description dependence of the finds. Researchers who refuse to be convinced by the evidence purportedly supporting it contest the very description of the relevant findings and offer altogether different framings for them.

UNIQUENESS

The Scrolls Jars, the Glass Assemblage, and the Hatchet

Additional framing puzzles have to do with the notion of uniqueness and with the related notions of centrality and marginality. What is one to make of a unique archaeological find? How central or how marginal to one's theory may one judge such an item to be? How can such a judgment be justified? And anyway, how unique is unique? That is, how unparalleled or unprecedented does a finding have to be for its uniqueness to serve as a premise in argumentation? Besides, isn't there an ever-present possibility in archaeology that today's claim of uniqueness will collapse with tomorrow's new finding? Furthermore, any claim about the uniqueness of a find may in a sense amount to an admission of failure to find more of the same, whether this is attributable to lack of diligence or to bad luck.

Take the case of the cylindrical jars, in which several of the scrolls were discovered and which are hence often referred to as "scrolls jars." Such jars were found not only in the scrolls caves but also at the site of Khirbet Qumran. Indeed, in the very first season of excavations at Qumran, de Vaux and Harding found an intact cylindrical jar, sunk into the floor of one of the rooms, which was identical with the scrolls jars of Cave 1. These jars are

Scrolls jars from Cave 1
© The Israel Museum, Jerusalem / by Avraham Hai

tall and cylindrical in shape, have a wide mouth, a low neck, no handles, and bowl-shaped lids. These and other features distinguish the Qumran jars from the bag-shaped storage jars commonly found at other Judaean sites of the first century BCE and first century CE. They are clearly rather rare and in any case distinctive of the geographical area of the Dead Sea (no such jars were found in Jerusalem). Still, a number of "similar" jars were found in nearby Jericho, some are reported in Masada, and one was reportedly found at Quailba, near ancient Abila in northern Jordan (Magness, 2002, pp. 70–89).[34] What are we to make of this?

---

34   Magness cites data from a 1998 Hebrew University M.A. thesis (in Hebrew) by Rachel Bar-Nathan on the pottery from the Herodian palaces at Jericho (Magness, 2002, pp. 80–81). It is not quite clear however whether more than one jar was found in Jericho that exactly matches the type of the scrolls jars of Qumran; mentioned also are possibly similar examples found at Masada. About the exemplar from Abila, Magness states that "unfortunately it is not illustrated" (p. 81).

The mainstream view, following de Vaux, emphasizes the identity between the pottery from the caves and that found in the ruins, as well as the autonomous and unique (or near unique) nature of this pottery. Scholars of the mainstream view cite these features as evidence in support of the hypothesis about the link between the caves and the site of Qumran. That is, the cylindrical jars play an important role in the argument that one and the same community inhabited the site (where its members wrote and copied the scrolls) and made use of the caves (where they stored them). Some lip service is being paid to the possible exceptions that may undermine the claim of the jars to uniqueness, but essentially these exceptions are minimized, explained away or ignored.[35] In contrast, a couple of minority esoteric views choose to focus precisely on the exceptions and make them a cornerstone in their theorizing. P. W. Lapp (1961) takes the Abila exception to establish that Abila became a place of refuge for the inhabitants of Qumran after the final destruction of the site in 68 CE. For Cansdale (1997), the Jericho jars are evidence in support of her contention that Qumran was an outpost controlled and operated by priests from Jericho.[36]

Consider now the finds of glass fragments. De Vaux's only reference to the glass finds at Qumran, in a preliminary report of 1953, is (in translation from the French) that "the fragments of glass are insignificant." In his book he does not mention glass at all. So the glass finds, at least until quite recently, could be considered unique, or exceptional. For the majority of scholars, following de Vaux, this was good enough reason to ignore the

---

35   See de Vaux, 1973, p. 33, n. 2; pp. 54–55, n. 1. (But note that de Vaux was not aware of the Jericho find.) Strikingly, in a footnote de Vaux acknowledges the following: "The pottery of Qumran now appears less 'autonomous' or 'original' than I stated it to be at an earlier stage" (p. 30, n. 2). He does not, however, proceed to draw any conclusion from this.

36   Thomas Kuhn's notion of "anomaly" comes to mind in connection with the use scholars try to make of "exceptions" in effecting a shift from an existing paradigm to a new one (Kuhn, 1962). Indeed it is quite evident to anyone who reads Norman Golb's book, *Who Wrote the Dead Sea Scrolls?* (1995), that Golb sees his own task in Kuhnian terms, namely as bringing about "a paradigm shift" or a "revolution" in the field of Qumran studies. One of his chapters is called "The Qumran–Essene Theory: A Paradigm Reconsidered;" see also pp. 109, 110, 284.

glass finds as marginal. But there are others for whom the glass fragments are central, much in the spirit of the scriptural saying: "The stone which builders refused is become the head stone of the corner" (Psalms 118:22).

Since de Vaux did not bring the results of his excavations at Qumran between 1951 and 1956 to final publication, responsibility for completion of the task fell to Jean-Baptiste Humbert of the École Biblique in Jerusalem.[37] At his invitation, Robert Donceel and Pauline Donceel-Voûte examined the pieces of glass stored at the Rockefeller Museum in Jerusalem that, in their judgment, could be traced to the inventory of the Qumran artifacts. The conclusion they reached was that some of the glass was locally produced at Qumran and some was imported from outside (1994, pp. 7–9). Given that glass was quite a luxury product in the Second Temple era, the Donceel team adduces the findings of fine glassware as major evidence in support of their interpretation of the site of Qumran as an aristocratic, villa-like settlement. "It seems clear that the occurrence of this glass collection is hard to reconcile with the hypothesis of the presence at the Khirbet Qumran site of a community seeking detachment from worldly affairs and poverty. In this respect the question about the cost and rarity of the decorated glass objects at that period is significant" (Donceel et al., 1999–2000, p. 18).[38]

---

37   The first English volume of final reports, out of the projected series of five, has only recently appeared (Humbert and Chambon, 2003). I note in passing that the complaints voiced over the years about the "incredible delay in publication" of the fragments of Cave 4 ("which is nothing less than an academic scandal": Fitzmyer, 1992, p. 144) are well known. The mammoth task of publishing the entire scroll material, however, has now been practically completed (in forty volumes of the DJD series), whereas the kindred (and not less-eagerly awaited) task of publishing the final reports of the excavations is only now beginning to be executed.

38   The authors of this report note that it is "one of the paradoxes of the archaeological complex" of Qumran that none of its glass artifacts have ever been published (p. 9). There seem to be many problems associated with the study of the glass from Qumran. Most of the glass fragments are small splinters ("not even one goblet was sufficiently well conserved for it to be completely restored or unambiguously identified," p. 11). In addition, not only is glass difficult to date in general, but in the case of Qumran many of the glass fragments, especially of the recently found ones (in the excavations conducted by I. Magen and Y. Peleg between 1993 and 2003), originate from dump heaps. It is therefore difficult to determine whether these fragments belong to the relevant pre-68 CE period or whether they belong to the later period, when a Roman

Another item that was found in Qumran and deserves some attention is the iron hatchet discovered in Cave 11. This find is a curiosity that highlights the excitement, as well as the frustration, inherent in an archaeological find that remains a singular item. The hatchet is a tool well known to archaeologists. It is primarily used in carpentry, and its likes were discovered in Roman territory. There is therefore nothing special or surprising about the hatchet finding as such, but it may be brought into striking relief in light of the textual material.

In his description of the Essenes and their way of life, Josephus tells us that upon choosing to join the Essene community, novices are given three items: a hatchet, a loin-cloth, and a white garment. They are to use the hatchet to dig a foot-deep hole in a deserted spot each time they relieve themselves, and then "to cover it with their garment so as not to shame the light of God, thereafter using the dug-out earth to cover the hole." In doing so, they apply quite literally the biblical prescriptions regarding the purity of the camp. Although going to stool is a natural need for man, Josephus tells us that the Essenes "believed that this defiles the body and it is their habit to wash their flesh with water afterwards" (*War* 2 VIII 9:148–149.).[39]

The hatchet that was found in Cave 11 is consistent with Josephus'description. But what is the probative value of this find? It was a unique find at Qumran, yet given the pervasiveness of similar hatchets in ancient and Roman sites it cannot be seen as distinct to the Essene hypothesis. De Vaux acknowledges that "it cannot be proved that the hatchet which we found was a specifically Essene instrument." At the same time he remarks that "it is equally impossible to prove that it was not an Essene instrument" (1973, p. 133). Still, the very framing of this find in the context of Josephus' text is highly suggestive, and it fits well with the overarching presumption in favor of the Qumran–Essene hypothesis. This is very much in line with what was referred to earlier as the "Gestalt method" that

---

garrison occupied the site. It is quite clear that no clear-cut conclusions can be drawn from the glass assemblage, at least not before it is finally published.

39   For more on the toilet habits and sanitation practices of the Essenes, on toilets in the Roman world, and on the finding of a toilet at Qumran, see Magness, 2002, pp. 105–113.

treats all the affirming finds as mutually augmenting the hypothesis and as collectively confirming it, rather than merely as severally consistent with it (see p. 89 above).

Reflecting upon the cases of the jars, the glass assemblage, and the hatchet, we may make the following observations. As we saw earlier, when a find is consistent with the researchers' favorite theory, the confirmation bias will make them consider the find as supporting the theory. When the find is not merely consistent but also unique (as in the case of the hatchet), the researchers will tend to consider the support this finding lends to the theory all the more dramatic or striking. A find that is inconsistent with one's favorite theory, on the other hand, needs to be explained away. But when an inconsistent finding happens to be unique (as in the case of the glass fragments), it becomes that much easier for the researchers simply and safely to ignore it. In other words, unique items somehow seem to score extra points when they are positive, and to be more easily discarded when they are negative.

The situation is different for those researchers who oppose the mainstream theory and offer alternative, minority hypotheses. The anomalies, that is to say the findings that are unique as well as problematic for the dominant theory, quite naturally become the focal points for these researchers' own dissenting theories and quite often provide the pillars on which they stand. (The cases of Cansdale and the Donceel team cited above are cases in point.) Too often, however, the near-exclusive focus of the dissenting researchers on such "trump" items leads them to assign to these items overblown probative values. This focus likely also contributes to what sometimes looks like their cavalier disregard of other findings that do not quite fit in with the theories they offer as alternatives to the dominant theory.

The Copper Scroll

And finally, there is the Copper Scroll. Archaeologists discovered it in 1952, in Cave 3. It is a document written on – or rather chiseled into – sheets of metal riveted into the shape of a scroll. It was not until 1956 that the complete scroll was cut open (in Manchester, England) and read. Its text, originally found in two rolled pieces, is a list comprising some sixty-four treasures "with fantastic amounts of gold and silver" (Magness, 2002, p. 25) buried in the Judaean Desert. The amount of treasure and the hiding place of each one are specified. "From every point of view," comments de Vaux, "it is different from the generality of the manuscripts at Qumran. It is the only document engraved on metal and the only text in Mishnaic Hebrew [i.e., later than the Qumran Hebrew]. In content it does not conform to any of the literary *genres* attested at Qumran. It consists of a catalogue of treasures which are allegedly hidden throughout Palestine" (1973, p. 108). An expedition mounted by John Allegro in 1961 was the first in a series of efforts to discover the treasures mentioned in the Copper Scroll, all of which came to nothing.

The Copper Scroll is unique, exceptional, and puzzling. At first it was supposed, in line with the overall picture of Qumran, that it describes hidden Essene treasures. Then doubts began to creep up as to whether the ascetic Essenes could possess the kind of wealth that was listed in the scroll. Even if we allow for the possibility, suggested by some researchers, that the Essene community was wealthy, as its individual members were required to transfer their private property to the community (and subsequently to lead an ascetic life), the amount of treasures listed in the Copper Scroll is too fantastic to record the actual assets of the community. So the suggestion that gained currency was that the Copper Scroll was a work of fiction: that it is to be taken as a piece of Jewish folklore, and that the treasures it lists are imaginary.[40]

However, it was difficult to reconcile this suggestion with the fact that the treasure list was inscribed on such a valuable metal as copper. It also did not quite fit with the prosaic, non-literary style of the text. These considerations rather testified to the likelihood that the list was after all a genuine inventory, possibly quite important to its author.[41] Another hypothesis afloat was that the Copper Scroll belonged to Jerusalem Zealots rather than to the Essenes and that it was they who hid it in the cave.[42]

40   This was Milik's position (1959).
41   This was Allegro's position (1960).
42   This was Cecil Roth's position (1964–66).

Gradually however the idea became entrenched that the Copper Scroll listed the treasures of the Jerusalem Temple. These were buried, or perhaps they were intended to be buried, in the Judaean Desert because of the approach of the Romans.[43] This was an appealing idea. At the same time, it constituted something of an embarrassment to the champions of the Qumran–Essene hypothesis. It was not clear how they could account for the fact that the sectarians were entrusted with the secrets of the Temple treasures. After all, the sectarians' vigorous opposition to the Jerusalem priesthood, from which they had long separated, was well known.

Unless, of course, it could be claimed that the Copper Scroll was altogether unrelated to the Qumran community, despite the fact that it was found in a cave in which sectarian documents were also found. This, basically, is the position that de Vaux eventually came to espouse. Unlike the other scrolls found in Cave 3, the Copper Scroll was discovered in the outer part of the cave and not quite inside it. This circumstance should surely add to the other exceptional traits of the Copper Scroll enumerated above. It is also important to note that J. T. Milik, the editor of the scroll, finally dated it to as late as 100 CE,[44] that is to say, to some time well after the destruction of the Qumran community. In addition, this scroll appears to be the only one in the entire scrolls corpus in which words of Greek origin occur. This is reason enough for some scholars, but not for others, to conclude that the Copper Scroll does not belong to the Qumranic corpus (Broshi and Eshel, 2001, p. 314; Garcia Martinez, 2003, p. 144).

43 Two further hypotheses were: (a) the treasures belonged to the Bar-Kokhba rebels (135 CE); (b) the treasures represent contributions to the Temple collected after its destruction in 70 CE. In principle, then, scholars divide as to (1) whether the treasures recorded in the Copper Scroll are genuine or imaginary; (2) whether or not the scroll belonged to the Essenes; and (3) whether the scroll was hidden in the cave before or after the destruction of the Qumran community. The tenuous consensus that seems to have reigned until quite recently was that the Copper Scroll is an authentic record of ancient treasures which probably belonged to the Temple in Jerusalem and which dates from around the time of the destruction (68–70 CE); but see n. 47 below.

44 In his early publication of the Copper Scroll (in *DJD* 3), J. T. Milik dated it to about the middle of the first century CE, i.e., to some time before the destruction of the Qumran community. In his later work, however, Milik revised this estimate and dated the scroll to the end of the century, i.e., to some time well after the destruction of the Qumran community. This dating remains controversial.

De Vaux's own conclusion about the Copper Scroll is as follows. "It would be easier to explain the unique character of this document, so foreign to the outlook and preoccupations of the community, if it emanated from some other source and had been deposited at a later stage." The scroll could, for example, have originated in the priestly circles of the Jerusalem Temple and could have been brought for safekeeping to the cave at Qumran by some priests some time after the destruction of the Temple in 70 CE.

The case of the Copper Scroll, then, is in many ways a special one. It concerns a find whose singularity is such that the excavator feels compelled to resort to more drastic measures than explaining it away: he feels compelled in effect to explain it *out*. The chief advocate of the Qumran–Essene narrative gives up the attempt to accommodate this scroll within the narrative and chooses rather to relegate it outside of its provenance altogether. In doing so he in effect declares the Copper Scroll a veritable anomaly.

It is not surprising that there are other opinions. Norman Golb, who champions the Jerusalem origin of the Qumran scrolls, makes the Copper Scroll a centerpiece of his own theory. He also declares it the central ("most important") document of the entire Qumran collection. Golb believes that it records deposits, throughout the Judaean Desert, not only of the Temple treasures but also of writings and scrolls. He is of the opinion that the latter included in the first place the scrolls placed in the caves of Qumran. In addition, he believes that they also included the writings that were found in the vicinity of Jericho already in antiquity, as recorded by Origen (late second century) and by Timotheus (early ninth century).[45]

Golb devotes much space in his book to a detailed and dramatic discussion of the Copper Scroll (1995, pp. 117–130; *passim.*). For him the

---

45   From the writings of Origen, one of the Church Fathers, it appears that in the early years of the third century some Hebrew and Greek biblical books were found in a jar near Jericho. (Church historian Eusebius refers to the same finding.) Several centuries later, in a letter written around the year 800 to Sergius, the Metropolitan of Elam, Timotheus I, the Nestorian patriarch of Seleucia, tells of the discovery of Hebrew manuscripts, both biblical and non-biblical, in a cave near Jericho. See Golb, 1995; Magness, 2002.

track record of the way it was handled by the scholars who comprised the official Jerusalem team in charge of the scrolls research is telling. It illustrates, he believes, what he takes to be their grand conspiracy to protect the Qumran–Essene hypothesis beyond all bounds of scholarly reasonableness. His own framing of the find of the Copper Scroll is worth reproducing in full:

> We may thus reasonably infer that it only slowly dawned upon de Vaux, Milik and others in Jerusalem that the contents of the Copper Scroll, if taken at face value, represented a danger for the Qumran–Essene hypothesis. The four thousand wealth-eschewing Essenes of first-century AD Palestine could not have anything like the quantities of silver and other precious metals described in the text – nor could any other small sect. If the text was indeed an authentic autograph, its treasures could only have come from the Temple.... The possibility must have become suddenly apparent that the scrolls as a whole could be conceived of as having derived not from Qumran, but from Jerusalem itself. Convinced, however, that they must be right in their view that the Essenes had written the scrolls, and that this had been accomplished at Khirbet Qumran, the principal scroll team members decided to declare the text before them a work of *fiction* (1995, p. 120).

In the first decade after the first publications of the text of the Copper Scroll in the late 1950s, this scroll had been the focus of much scholarly scrutiny. Interest in it has later subsided, and again revived in the early 1980s.[46] Yet to this day it remains an enigma. Whatever one's favorite interpretation of the Copper Scroll, it must surely be accorded pride of place in any discussion of the notion of uniqueness and of the role of singular exemplars in archaeology.[47]

---

46 For a detailed history of research into the Copper Scroll until the 1990s see Wolters, 1994.

47 Eshel and Safrai (2002) have recently advanced a thesis meant to reduce the enigma. According to this thesis (1) the Copper Scroll is a sectarian document; (2) it lists fictitious treasures; (3) it reflects a contemporary folkloristic tradition of describing

In this chapter, I have attempted to work out the nature of the archaeological arguments connected with the Qumran hypothesis. Central to this analysis have been the implications of the fact that the excavation of Khirbet Qumran followed rather than preceded the discovery of the scrolls. Focusing on the logic of research actually employed by the practitioners, I have argued that the researchers presumed the Qumran–Essene theory to be true, unless and until proven otherwise. I have exposed and traced this "presumptive" approach against the backdrop of the Bayesian method which is the leading normative approach in the empirical sciences. In addition, I have portrayed the Qumran–Essene theory against the tumult of rival theories that offer dissenting alternative interpretations of the site.

From the ongoing controversy about the interpretation of the site of Qumran I have drawn the conclusion that, insofar as this controversy does not attest to the irrationality of some of the proponents of the various theories, it does attest to deep disagreements among them about the evidence. Further, I have shown that no agreement can be reached about the evidence because of an underlying interdependence between theory and evidence: both description and interpretation of crucial pieces of evidence depend on the theory from which the researcher sets out. This constitutes a methodological interpretive circle, additional to the substantive ones encountered in Chapter One. To illustrate and substantiate my claims, I discussed a number of specific pieces of evidence that play a role in the Qumran argument. The last portion of the chapter was devoted to questions of framing and uniqueness, as these two notions are particularly important for understanding how archaeological finds are implicated in an interpretive circle.

---

the hidden treasures of the first (not the second!) Jerusalem Temple; (4) as such the scroll is not so lacking in context after all: it belongs within an existing literary genre of which there are other exemplars.

CHAPTER THREE

Sects and Scholars

THE "SCROLLS SECT"

The answer to the question concerning the authorship of the Dead Sea scrolls had initially been: the sect of the Essenes. As critical questions about this assumption began to accumulate, it gradually became common practice to drop the presupposition about the Essene connection and treat this connection as a hypothesis that requires substantiation. The more neutral answer that replaced the initial one was that the authors of the scrolls belonged to the Qumran sect, or to the Dead Sea sect. This too was criticized for not being entirely free of presupposition either. As was pointed out, this answer still presupposes an immanent connection between the scrolls and the particular site near the caves in which they were found. This connection, argued the critics, should also be taken as a hypothesis that requires substantiation. And so the solution finally adopted by the scholarly community to the question of who wrote the scrolls was: the scrolls sect.

This answer is obviously no more than a circular and vacuous label. It fills its role as a reference, but tells us nothing about the identity of the authors of the scrolls and who they actually were. Yet even this vacuous-seeming label is, perhaps ironically, not altogether free of presupposition. It assumes that the authors of the scrolls were *sectarians*. And to the extent that the term "sect" is used advisedly and not loosely – i.e., to the extent that it is not used simply as interchangeable with "group" and its cognates – it has conceptual, methodological, and empirical implications. These implications and some of their ramifications are, broadly speaking, the concerns of this chapter.

What does the concept of a sect entail, and what is conceptually involved in the claim about the existence of a sect? What should characterize a group of people for it to qualify as a sect rather than, say, a party, a movement, a denomination, or an order? It is useful in reflecting on these questions to realize what may be entailed by the denial of the existence claim of a sect. One can deny that a group answering to a particular historical description ever existed, or claim that it existed as a group but was not a sect, or indeed claim that there were several sects involved rather than just one.

What then are our initial, theoretical, expectations from a sect, and does the present state of Dead Sea Scrolls research permit us to conclude that these expectations are indeed fulfilled in the case at hand? Is there textual justification for identifying the group we are dealing with, qua sect, with another, better known, sect? Or is the nature of the enterprise rather to identify the scrolls group independently as a singular sect, not to be identified with any other one? Moreover, the notion of a sect, or *heterodoxy*, presupposes in principle the existence of an *orthodoxy*. If this is the case, are we in a position to ascertain that orthodoxy did indeed exist in the two centuries preceding the destruction of Jerusalem? And are we in a position to determine its main religious contours? What can be said about the specific nature of the sect's separation from the mainstream and about the religious energy that fueled it?

These are some of the questions that, while being conceptually motivated, require empirical answers. Some of the empirical answers may simply not be forthcoming, for there is so much that we do not know and may never know. But some empirical answers have been offered during the decades of Dead Sea Scrolls research, and these may stand in need of conceptual scrutiny. Other answers may yet be given, once greater conceptual clarity is attained.

WHY "SECT"?

When the very first scrolls from the Dead Sea had been discovered and read, they were immediately pronounced to be sectarian in nature. At the same time they were conjectured to be of Essene origin. The sectarian library of the Essenes, the sectarian beliefs of the Essenes, the sectarian way of life of the Essenes – these notions became entrenched in Dead Sea Scrolls research from its earliest stages.

The sectarian nature of the archaeological find at the site of Qumran is at the heart of the Qumran–Essene hypothesis. And as we saw, much of the controversy surrounding Dead Sea Scrolls research has to do with the identification of the Qumran settlement as a sectarian center. Interest in the issue of the sectarian center, it may be well to bear in mind, extends beyond the material point of view, be it geographical or archaeological. It has to do rather with the very notion of monastic life, so central to Christianity, and with the conjecture that the correct interpretation of the site of Qumran may be offering us a glimpse into its point of origin. While the story of early Christianity is to a large extent one of monks and saints who isolate themselves in the desert, the evidence we have about the institutionalization of this desert existence within collective monastic structures governed by strict rules and rituals starts relatively late, only in the second and third centuries CE. The stakes, then, are high.

Three ancient authors are our main sources of knowledge about the Essenes. Let us look more closely at how they describe the group of people they refer to as Essenes, with a particular focus on the notion of sectarianism. For Philo of Alexandria the Essenes are a "portion" of the people (*Every Good Man is Free*, 75:12–13). For Pliny the Elder they are a solitary "tribe" or "people" (*gens sola*) (*Natural History* 5:15.73). For Josephus Flavius the Essenes are a "heresy" (*hairesis*), a term that is usually rendered as "philosophy" or "school of thought," and is sometimes rendered as "sect" (*War* 2 VIII 1:119).[1]

It is worth noting, however, that Josephus applies the same label of "heresy" to the other two major groups or parties he discusses, namely the Pharisees and the Sadducees (ibid.).[2] So, if one wishes to base one's reference to the Essenes as a "sect" on Josephus, one would have to refer

---

1 Etymologically, the Greek term *hairesis* connotes both a choice and the thing chosen. The meaning has been narrowed to the selection of religious or political doctrines, or adhesion to parties in Church or State.

2 Note that in the English version of the New Testament the Pharisees and the Sadducees are referred to sometimes as "heresies" and sometimes as "sects"; e.g., Acts 5:17, 15:5, 24:5, 26:5.

to the Pharisees and to the Sadducees as sects as well. But the very point of the scholarly reference to the Essenes as a sect is to distinguish them thereby from the Pharisees and the Sadducees. "Josephus' presentation of the Pharisees, the Sadducees, and the Essenes as philosophies or as parties is somewhat misleading," says Stendahl. "The former may adequately be described as parties" (1992, p. 7).

One question, then, is whether the uncritical, yet common, designation of the Essenes as a sect is justified. This would call for more than a close study of the Essenes: it would require exploring what is implied by being a sect. Irrespective of this question, however, one has to bear in mind that the identity between the authors of the scrolls and the Essenes is a matter of dispute. And even if it weren't a matter of dispute but rather one of general consensus, the assertion of this identity would still have to be based on argumentation rather than taken for granted. As was pointed out at the outset, many scholars in the field have taken to referring to the authors of the scrolls and their community in a neutral, non-committal manner as the "Dead Sea sect" or the "Qumran sect," rather than as the Essenes (Schiffman, 1992, p. 40; 1994, *passim*).

While these designations are helpful in fending off the charge of prejudging the Essene connection, they still leave open the charge of prejudging the sectarian issue. The question still has to be addressed whether the composers and copiers of the scrolls, and their community, were sectarians. And this issue has to be approached independently of the question whether the Essenes were the authors of the scrolls. That is to say, one ought to look at the internal evidence of the scrolls. One ought to look at the testimony of the texts themselves in order to come to a conclusion as to whether or not the scrolls are the product of a sect, whichever sect it may be – keeping an open mind about the possibility that the scrolls may be the product of more than just one sect. In addition, as we have seen, the connection between the scrolls and the settlement of Qumran is itself the focus of dispute. So, arguments must be presented independently for each of the three sides of the Essenes–scrolls–Qumran triangle. The notion of a sect is central to them all.

In his early book *The Hidden Scrolls from the Judaean Desert*, Yadin is aware of the problem:

Had the discoveries in the Dead Sea caves been confined to Biblical books alone, it is doubtful whether we should now have any information about the community whose scribes copied the holy works.... We would not even have been able to assume that the books belonged to a particular sect and not just to ordinary inhabitants of the area in which they were discovered.

Taking a first crack at addressing this problem, Yadin continues:

These writers...were people who had serious complaints against the inhabitants of Jerusalem and their priests, and their Teacher of Righteousness was persecuted and had been compelled to flee from the Wicked Priest. But from these books alone it would not be possible to establish with finality that these people constituted a special religious sect. (1992, p. 113)

From this passage we see that for Yadin the elements of religious dissent and of being persecuted carry weight in determining that one is dealing with a "special religious sect." At the same time, he says that these elements are not quite sufficient to allow one to infer this "with finality." From the way Yadin continues we learn that for him the conclusion about the sectarian nature of the group in question was clinched by the discovery of the scroll referred to as the *Rule of the Community* (or the *Manual of Discipline*). This scroll details a code of behavior for the members of the group as well as a penal code, and also basic articles of faith and a method of initiating new members into the group. Clearly, for Yadin there is no question that this means that this particular scroll is of, for, and by a sect.

The sectarian nature of the authors – as well as of the audience – of the Dead Sea scrolls must be considered in the first instance, as was pointed out, by focusing on the textual evidence of the scrolls themselves. In the above passages Yadin does just that. His approach contrasts with an alternative one that was favored by some of the scrolls researchers. The starting point of the alternative approach is equating the scrolls community with the Essenes. It then proceeds to apply to the scrolls community everything that the ancient writers tell us about the Essenes. But regardless of the respective merit of each approach, neither will get us far if we do not have some conception of what it is that we are looking for. That is to say, we have to have some idea of what it is to be a sect, of what it is that distinguishes a religious sect from a party, a movement, a denomination, or an order. We need to be more informed about what are its defining or characteristic features.

TO BE A SECT

Traits Shared by Sects

The portrait of a sect that emerges from the literature relates essentially to the sect form that is known to have asserted itself in Christian culture early in the middle ages.[3] It relates to an ideal-type of sect, according to which it is a form of social organization of a relatively small-sized society of strict believers. The members of the sect live apart from the world in some way and express defiance of it or withdrawal from it. They are characterized as possessing a spirit of austerity and asceticism, as well as of segregation and militancy. A sect will thus typically embody a posture of rejection. It will be a protest group, a religious or a non-religious form of protest of the disinherited of the earth. As such its members often develop a polar worldview, seeing the world in terms of bad and good or black and white, with no shades of gray. Their antagonistic, Manichaean mentality typically divides the world into the few elect good, "We," and the many condemned bad, "Them."

All sects are said to be extremely dominating of the lives of their membership. The ideological or religious domination that sects exercise over their members is supported by measures that control most, if not all, aspects of their lives. Thus sects are often set apart by endogamy, by rigorous morality and over-strict observance, by distinct rules and habits of eating and abstinence, by peculiarities of dress, by limitations on contacts with outsiders, and by refusal to participate in common activities and practices of the mainstream society.

With time, many sects lose their antagonistic or withdrawn posture vis-à-vis the outside world and undergo a process of "routinization." Those that do not undergo such a process become established sects which

3   The *locus classicus* is Troeltsch, 1931.

typically divide into separatist and non-separatist ones. The separatists secede from the world in a literal geographic sense and live as a total community in territorial isolation. The non-separatists attempt to maintain their separateness from and their opposition to the general society while remaining within it.[4]

The origin and formation of sects is associated not just with religious and ideological concerns but with social and political interests as well. Also, the origin of a sect is often associated with a charismatic leader. A sect is typically formed by an initiator, a leader who impresses his own vision upon the group and lays down the formative patterns for the behavior and beliefs of its members. According to their ideological orientation, sects divide into several types, among which are conversionist, which actively seek to convert the rest of the world and thereby to change it, and adventist, characterized by the constant expectation of drastic divine intervention and of a new dispensation.

Sectarian Traits of the Dead Sea Group

The phenomenon of sectarianism happens to be of much interest in the political and religious reality at the dawn of the twenty-first century. The textbook description of sects delineated above may be felt to be too old-fashioned and narrow to cover everything that we would want to associate with the phenomenon of sectarianism today. But there can be little doubt that this description resonates remarkably well with material contained in the major scrolls from the Dead Sea: those usually referred to as distinctly sectarian, notably the *Rule of the Community*, the *Damascus Covenant* and the *War scroll*. The *Temple scroll* may also be added to this list.

Thus, these texts attest in a striking manner to the withdrawal of the group from the world, to its rejection of the world and its defiance against it. Moreover, they record the group's vehement protest against the Jerusalem priesthood. It is this protest, many scholars believe, that was

---

4   Mary Douglas (2001, chapter 2) discusses yet another, interesting subcategory of sects called *enclave*. For some, the category of an enclave is the comprehensive one: not every enclave is a sect but all sects (of the Jewish/Christian/Moslem sort) are enclaves.

the impetus for the group's separation from the mainstream community. The texts also document the group's highly stringent demands regarding religious observance, as well as its ascetic code of behavior. They exhibit a fierce "we–them" mode of relating to the world that is couched in the formative theological picture of the Sons of Light against the Sons of Darkness. Moreover, the documents in question are permeated throughout by a sense of the total domination exercised by the group over all aspects of its members' lives. We learn from them that this domination starts even before the candidates become full members of the group, during their two or three years of probation, and does not quite end even when a member is expelled from the group for transgressing any of its rules.[5]

Of central importance, too, is the role of the presumed founder and leader of the group, the fabled and elusive figure of the Teacher of Righteousness. Hints about him are strewn in the three scrolls mentioned above, but even more so in two *Commentaries* (*Habakkuk* and *Nahum*) and in the *Thanksgiving Hymns*. Evidence reconstructed from these hints adds up to the following picture. The Teacher of Righteousness lived some time around the middle of the second century BCE. Persecuted by an "Evil Priest" (possibly Jonathan who was appointed High Priest in Jerusalem in 152 BCE: Eshel, 1997, p. 89), he apparently led the group into exile in the north ("Damascus"). The Teacher possessed religious genius that expressed itself primarily in his divinely inspired commentaries on biblical texts. He died a violent death at the hands of his enemies.

We can see that there is much correspondence between the features of the scrolls community as they emerge from the scrolls texts and the generally accepted picture of sects as delineated by the sociological literature. It may not be idle to recall at this point that there is also a large degree of correspondence between what Josephus tells us about the Essenes and the sociologically delineated picture of sects. Reference to the authors and audience of the scrolls as sectarians, therefore, seems to be eminently

5   An intriguing speculation in this connection is that John the Baptist, who subsisted on a diet of grasshoppers and wild honey (Matt. 3:4), might have been a lapsed or expelled member of the Dead Sea sect who was still bound by the dietary vows he made upon admittance to the sect (Broshi, 2004b, n. 13 and further references there; see also Flusser, 1997, p. 95 and further references there).

justified – and the identification of the scrolls community with the Essenes hardly avoidable. Two additional issues, however, have caused anxiety and debate among scholars in this connection. They relate to celibacy and to the question of geographic separation.

Celibacy and Geographic Center

It is doubtful whether either of these issues would have been raised on the basis of the texts of the scrolls alone. They have become important primarily because they loom large in what the ancient authors tell us about the Essenes. There was pervasive scholarly desire to establish an identity between the celibate Essenes, as described by these writers, and the scrolls sect. There was also pervasive scholarly desire to establish Qumran as the geographic center of the scrolls sect. These two academic aspirations brought the two issues into prominence, even though neither celibacy nor a separate geographic center bears crucially on the question of sectarianism as such, in the sense of being necessary conditions for it. Note, however, that there is asymmetry here. Had the scrolls contained compelling reference to celibacy, this would settle the matter of seeing the scrolls community as a sect. But the absence of such reference need not settle the matter in the opposite direction.

Concerning celibacy, let us consider in turn what we learn from the ancient authors, from the scrolls, and from the archaeological finds. Pliny and Philo both write explicitly that the Essenes did not marry.[6] Josephus says this too, describing women as "wanton" and saying that no woman "keeps her plighted troth to one man" (*War* 2 VIII 2:120–121). But he also reports that one group, or "order," of the Essenes did not shun marriage and took wives in order to propagate (ibid. VIII 13:160–161). When we turn our attention to the scrolls, it turns out that no direct endorsement of celibacy emerges from them, nor do they provide evidence that the scrolls community was

---

6   Pliny the Elder describes the Essenes as a people "unique of its kind...without women
     and renouncing love entirely" (*Natural History* 5.73). Philo says that "no one of the
     Essenes ever marries a wife" and that the Essenes "repudiate marriage; and at the same
     time they practise continence in an eminent degree" (*Hypothetica* 11.14). Magness
     takes these writers, as well as Josephus, to display a pronounced misogynistic bias
     (2002, pp. 163–164).

celibate.[7] As for archaeology, let us first note that it is difficult to imagine what material findings could in principle directly corroborate a thesis about the celibacy of a community inhabiting any site. It is much easier however to say what material findings would be helpful in establishing the presence of women in a particular settlement. A significant finding of what scholars nowadays refer to as "gendered objects," such as jewelry, combs, mirrors, cosmetics, and also spinning whorls and shafts, would attest to the presence of women. (In Masada more than three hundred and eighty spindle whorls were found!) The finding of no gendered objects at all would at best invoke an argument from silence, for what it's worth. And the finding of just a few such items leaves the arena open to interpretations and speculations.

The archaeological finds at Qumran that relate to the possible presence of women are considered and analyzed in great detail by Magness (2002, pp. 175–179). She concludes that only one spindle whorl and possibly four beads can be identified with any certainty as gendered objects from the relevant contexts of the Qumran site – even though she acknowledges that none of her conclusions "can be considered definitive" until the final publication of the material from de Vaux's excavations. Her verdict is that "the archeological evidence suggests only minimal female presence at Qumran" (ibid., p. 175). Yet, since this is based on an argument from silence, Magness points out that "it is impossible to prove *on the basis of the archaeological evidence alone* that women were not present and active in various capacities" (ibid., p. 179, emphasis in original).[8]

---

7   The *Community Rule*, 1QS (or *Manual of Discipline*), does not refer to women, and yet it mentions "fruitfulness of seed" among the blessings of the virtuous Sons of Light (1QS 4.7). Any conclusion drawn from this as to whether or not this text advocates celibacy must therefore be an argument from silence. Yadin, for example, says that the sect "does not oppose the marriage of its members," yet in discussing the *Manual* he adds (without quoting) that, "within the sect itself there were groups of members who refrained from marrying" (1992a, p. 174). Other sectarian documents, however, do contain regulations referring to women and children (e.g., the *Messianic Rule*: 1QSa 1.4–5, the *Damascus Covenant*: CD 7.6–9, the *War Scroll*: 1QM 7.3).

8   Hirschfeld challenges Magness' conclusion and verdict. He mentions needles, combs, cosmetic vessels, and fibulae (see 2003a, p. 652; 2003b, p. 36). Eshel (2003, p. 58) and Broshi (2003, p. 66) contest Hischfeld's points. (They point out, inter alia, that

In addition of course the problem of the skeletons of women and children found in the cemetery has to be contended with. "Clearly," says de Vaux, "the women's tombs do not strengthen the argument that the community was related to the Essenes, but they do not rule it out either" (1973, p. 48). This issue was discussed above, in Chapter Two (see especially n. 15 and accompanying text). As we saw, recent research suggests the possibility that all the skeletons of women and children found in the subsidiary cemeteries at Qumran are relatively recent Bedouin burials.

Celibacy is not among the characterizing features of a religious sect in general: it is, however, a central characterizing feature of a *monastic order*. A monastic order is typically taken to be a protest group that does not sever itself from the older established body of church or orthodoxy but remains within it. Monastic orders often exhibit features that are associated with sectarian qualities, such as the practice of austerity and asceticism, employment of segregating rules, peculiarities of dress, and more (O'Dea, 1968). But still, a monastic order as such is not a sect. So those who would see the scrolls community as a celibate sect and Qumran as a monastery have to shoulder a rather specific burden. They have to make clear whether they regard the Qumran community in sectarian or in monastic terms, or perhaps in both. They also have to work out further the implications of their chosen position with respect to the interpretation of the texts as well as of the archaeological find.

Regarding the question of geographic segregation, the textual evidence from the scrolls seems inconsistent, and is in any case inconclusive. The *Rule of the Community* is commonly taken to provide a code of behavior aimed at a single community leading a communal life, like that of a kibbutz or a monastery, within a territorially isolated compound. The *Damascus Covenant*, on the other hand, seems to address a plurality of communities that are dispersed in "camps."[9] However, as was noted earlier, geographic

---

only one comb from the relevant period was found at Qumran and that anyway, since combs were used mainly to remove lice, they are not necessarily "gendered objects" and could have belonged to men.)

9   Similar discrepancies occur in what the ancient sources tell us about the Essenes. The famous passage from Pliny (discussed in Chapter One) locates them on the western

separation is not, as such, a defining feature of a sect, which may be separatist or non-separatist in geographic terms.

The question whether it is a geographically isolated community that the scrolls address, or rather communities that are dispersed in cities, is certainly of considerable intrinsic interest. A geographically isolated center in the desert may provide an early, nascent model for the kind of collective, ritualized, spiritual life that developed into the monastic movement which was to become so important in the history of Christianity. Nevertheless, the issue of the sectarian nature of the scrolls community (or communities) does not hinge on an answer to the question as posed.

Some scholars believe that in reality the community of the scrolls combined both the separatist and the non-separatist models.[10] That is to say, they believe that this community may have had a communal center, possibly at Qumran, but that it also had adherents who were dispersed in "camps" in many Judaean towns and villages. If this possibility is considered plausible it may be further surmised that there could have been some traffic between center and periphery. Men could go down to the desert, perhaps leaving their families behind (but then again, perhaps taking some family members along), for a period of study and spiritual renewal.

WHICH SECT?

The discussion thus far has focused on general features characteristic of religious sects and common to many of them, in an attempt to examine whether they apply to the Dead Sea group as well. On the whole we saw that such a match does exist. But above and beyond these largely typological and sociological points, the spiritual dimension of the Dead

---

shore of the Dead Sea, above Engedi ("below them Engada"). Dio Chrisostom (c. 40–112 CE) mentions the Essenes in "a very blessed city situated near the Dead Water" [sic] (see Stern, 1974, pp. 538–539). However, Josephus says they live in "every town" (*War* 2 VIII 4:124), and Philo says they live only in villages, or in many towns (*Hypothetica* 11.1).

10 Notably Shemaryahu Talmon and David Flusser.

Sea group has to be explored. Questions must be addressed that relate to the highly particular ideational mettle of this highly particular sect. The purportedly distinctive sectarian nature of the Dead Sea Scrolls community is the focus of many scholarly debates and controversies. If it is claimed to be a sect, does this imply heterodoxy? If it does, then is the further implication justified – namely that orthodoxy existed at the time, against which the sect protested? Against whom then did it protest and from whom did it separate? What was the nature of its protest? What passion animated the protest and kept fueling it?

Heterodoxy and Orthodoxy

The antagonistic posture of a sect – any sect – is typically portrayed as directed against a dominant orthodoxy. The orthodoxy of the day is taken, from the point of view of the sect, to embody institutional religion and accommodation to the world. With regard to the Dead Sea sect, the tantalizing question is whether indeed orthodoxy existed during its lifetime. Was there already a recognized religious mainstream? More specifically, the question is whether there was a mainstream that functioned as a kind of "default option" for any Jew born in Palestine in the two centuries preceding the destruction of the Temple. It is not at all clear that this question, as posed, is not anachronistic. It is also not clear that the claim of a sectarian existence is not problematically retrodictive.

What is clear is that some time *after* the destruction of the Temple in Jerusalem an orthodoxy in religious Jewish life gradually established itself. The tradition of the Sages emerged in Yavneh soon after the fall of Jerusalem to the Romans. Rabbinic, halakhic, normative Judaism as we know it today, and which has occupied center stage in Jewish life for almost two millennia, is a direct product and continuation of this tradition. This orthodoxy embodies the triumph of the faction of the Pharisees over all its rivals. The Sadducees, whose source of power and *raison d'être* was the Temple service, did not survive the destruction of the Temple and disappeared for good from world history soon thereafter.

The period prior to the destruction – i.e., the period just preceding the beginning of the Christian era – is among the most extensively researched eras in Antiquity. Still, whether or not there was a dominant party in the life of Palestinian Jews before the destruction is an issue that has not been settled, let alone whether it was the Pharisees or the Sadducees. And the question whether or not there was religious orthodoxy at the time is importantly related to yet another unsettled issue, namely, whether the biblical canon already existed before the destruction of the Temple. It is a well documented fact that this was a period of great religious fermentation marked by the existence and activity of a large number of religious movements, groups, "heresies," or sects. Whether any of these religious groups enjoyed hegemony over the others is not only an open question, it is also a loaded one. It does not really ask which of the groups was more popular with the majority of the people: we are not dealing with a democracy in this case. The question, rather, is about where the locus of power resided, and what its relationship to the major parties was.

Political Power and Religious Power

A distinction must be drawn between the locus of political power and the locus of religious power. Political power at this time was in the hands of the Hasmonean kings, who ultimately derived their power from the external source of the Seleucid Hellenistic dynasty. They were not dependent for their power, therefore, on the endorsement of either of the two major parties, the Pharisees and the Sadducees.

The Hasmonean kings were not consistent in their attitude toward the Pharisees and the Sadducees. The historical record seem to suggest that they shifted their alliances and allegiances from one to the other. The struggle between the Sadducees and the Pharisees is believed to have begun during the reign of John Hyrcanus, 135–104 BCE, who first tended toward the Pharisees but toward the end of his life switched to the side of the Sadducees; Alexander Jannaeus (and perhaps John Hyrcanus II) supported the Sadducees.

Religious power was in the hands of the high priesthood which was responsible for the holy work in the Temple and it was from this that it derived its power base. The historical record here attests to a complex picture. The high priests traditionally belonged to the family of Zadok. However, during the period in question not all high priests were members of this privileged priestly family. The Hasmonean kings, for their own political reasons, deprived the Zadokite family of the exclusive privileges of high priesthood that it is traditionally believed to have held for some eight hundred years. (This remains a debatable point among scholars, however: some maintain that the Hasmoneans themselves may have been Zadokite.)

Another complicating factor is that it is not even altogether clear that the members of the Zadokite dynasty were Sadducees in their political or religious affiliations.[11] In fact, some seem to have embraced the Pharisee persuasion. The picture that emerges is that the center of religious power in the Jerusalem Temple shifted in more than one sense. It shifted back and forth between high priests who belonged to the Zadokite family and those who did not, and it shifted between the Sadducees, who probably held it most of the time, and the Pharisees, who appear to have held it some of the time.

Protest Against Whom?

The upshot of all of this is the following: There is a standard view about what is implied, explicitly or implicitly, when a certain group of people is designated as a religious "sect." The implication seems to be that there exists a hegemonic religious dogma, a recognized religious mainstream, or an established religious orthodoxy against which the group in question protests and from which it secedes. As was shown, the picture that emerges from the preceding discussion regarding the existence of a hegemonic religious orthodoxy in the relevant period is ambiguous. So for some scholars the question remains whether the Dead Sea group can be regarded, strictly speaking, as a religious sect. At the same time, it is quite clear that the story of the Dead Sea group does involve both protest and secession. The target of both acts, as we saw, is likely to have been not an established religious orthodoxy as such; it seems, rather, to have been the priestly circles in charge of the holy work in the Jerusalem Temple.

---

11 It is possible that the name "Sadducees" derives from the fact that members of the Zadokite priestly family were among its founding members. It cannot be assumed, however, that all Zadokites joined the politico-religious party of the Sadducees, or that all Sadducees belonged to the Zadokite family (Main, 2000).

There can be no doubt that much, perhaps most, of the protest of the Dead Sea group as recorded in the scrolls is on matters of priestly purity. From the point of view of the scrolls' authors, the Temple in particular and Jerusalem in general had become an abomination. The priestly work of the Temple, the supreme locus of purity and holiness, became impure in their eyes. The fervor of the denouncement is unequivocal. The "they" whom the sectarians reject cannot be seen as merely mistaken or wrong: they are accused of arrogance and sinful defilement. The precise identity of the "they," however, is a matter of scholarly debate. It is in fact closely linked with the question of the identity of the Dead Sea sect, or community, itself.

Sadducees or Pharisees?

One of the last major scrolls to be published is *Miqsat Ma'ase Ha-Torah*, 4QMMT (see Chapter One, pp. 56–58).[12] This text, sometimes referred as the *Halakhic Letter*, is a polemical letter written as a personal epistle to a high-ranking person in Jerusalem concerning halakhic matters. A striking feature of this scroll is that it contains a declaration of secession from the majority of the people (*"parashnu merov ha'am,"* meaning "we have segregated ourselves from the majority of the people"). There is broad consensus among scholars nowadays that it was the Hasmonean seizure of the office of high priest that led to the withdrawal of Zadokite priests from the Temple and to the founding of the Dead Sea community. Still, there is scholarly dispute as to whether the brunt of the sectarians' protest was directed first and foremost against the illegitimacy of the usurping Jerusalem priests or against their personal apostasy, their ethical conduct, and perhaps most importantly, against the laxity of their ritual practices (Schwartz, 1992, p. 178; Eshel, 1997, p. 89; Kugler, 2000, p. 691).

The *Halakhic Letter* lists some twenty-two rules, or commandments, over whose interpretation the seceding group disagrees with the addressee of the scroll. Several of these rules are prefaced by a phrase such as "we say"

12   The "composite text" of *Miqsat Ma'ase ha-Torah* ('Some Works of the Law'; 4QMMT) was compiled by Qimron and Strugnell (1994). (For more on the compilation of this text, see Introduction, above).

or "we think," indicating controversy. Thus: "And also concerning flowing liquids, we say that in these there is no purity. Even flowing liquids cannot separate unclean from clean moisture." And again: "And also concerning lepers. We say that they should not enter the holy purity." The interpretation of these rules that is attacked by the author of the scroll – invariably as too lenient – is known to coincide with the Pharisaic interpretation. Some have concluded from this that the seceding group, whether or not one wishes to identify it with the Essenes of the ancient authors, was an offshoot of the Sadducees and that its protest was directed against the Pharisees (see Sussmann, 1994, pp. 187–191).[13]

This inference, however, is problematic. It has to be borne in mind that the Pharisees started out as a party of reform motivated largely by social and political concerns. On general principles it is to be expected that a sect – any religious sect – of a fundamentalist, purist persuasion will incline toward more ancient and "authentic" versions and interpretations of the relevant laws and commandments. On general principles it is to be expected therefore that the members of the scrolls community, ferocious in their strict observance of the biblical commandments, would posture themselves in opposition to the Pharisaic interpretation of the *halakhah*. But this in itself does not warrant the conclusion that this community was aligned with the party of the Sadducees or was its offshoot.

Indeed, a number of passages in the scrolls corpus express views that are contrary to Sadducean doctrines. For example, the scrolls attest to a belief in the immortality of the soul, contrary to the Sadducean belief that the soul perishes with the body. So also in the matter of spirits and angels, in whose existence the sectarians believe but the Sadducees do not. These and other examples led to some early scholarly verdicts that the Dead Sea sect was Pharisaic (Ginzberg called them "hyper Pharisees"). At the same time and from an altogether different angle, one may bring to bear on the issue at hand the well-known phenomenon of the "narcissism of small

---

13   J. Baumgarten provides a list of elements common to the *halakhah* of the Qumran sect, on the one hand, and to the Pharisaic *halakhah*, on the other, mostly according to the text of the *Damascus Document*. His overall conclusion, nevertheless, is that the Qumran sect was not Pharisaic in its outlook (1997, p. 97).

differences." The suggestion, based on psychological insight and evidence that goes back to a 1918 comment by Freud, is that sects tend to direct their most vehement attacks against those closest to them ideologically but who diverge from them in matters which outsiders might consider minutiae. If this is the case and if it is by and large against the Pharisees that the Dead Sea sect turns most passionately, are we not perhaps to surmise that it is a Pharisaic variant after all?

This should amount to recognition that the scholarly attempts to establish that the scrolls community was "really" an offshoot of either the Sadducees or the Pharisees cannot be conclusively supported by the existing historical and textual material. Sussmann makes the point that a variety of "popular classes and fanatical religious sects" were active during the Second Commonwealth, who waged what he describes as a dual battle: "a religious–*political* struggle (ethical and social) against the priestly Sadducean aristocracy, on the one hand, and a religious–*halakhic* struggle against the opponents of the strict Sadducean tradition (i.e., the Pharisees), on the other" (1994, p. 194; see Chapter One, p. 57) In other words, it is all too easy here to conflate social and political concerns together with religious concerns. The fact that in the scrolls there is opposition to Pharisaic renderings of halakhic rules does not in and of itself justify relegating the authors of the scrolls to the Sadducean social-political camp, and vice versa.

The Pharisees were in conflict with Sadducees and Zadokites, namely with the priestly aristocratic families in Jerusalem, over matters concerning the Temple service. At the same time they were in conflict with various halakhically strict, separatist, sometimes rebellious, groups and sects over matters concerning the interpretation of the Law. From the point of view of the Pharisees every opposition, whether on social–political grounds or on religious–halakhic grounds, is given the derogatory label of "Sadducees." And as was pointed out earlier, it is the Pharisaic point of view that eventually gained the upper hand and became the normative Jewish point of view. In light of all of this, it is consistent with everything we know to regard the scrolls community as a spiritual and separatist sect – possibly the Essenes of the non-rabbinic literature – that is halakhically close to the Sadducees yet distancing itself socially from the Sadducees and engaged in bitter conflict with them over matters concerning the Temple service.

It is an understandable desire of scholars to gain as much insight as they possibly can into the scrolls community. For some of them, however, this means insistence on making it an offshoot of some other group with which they feel greater familiarity. But instead of pursuing this endeavor of identifying the scrolls sect *with* a different and presumably more familiar group, an alternative strategy might prove more fruitful (see Chapter One, p. 32). The alternative strategy would be not to prejudge the issue but to focus on identifying the sect in and of itself, through exposing and exploring its own most distinctive traits, insofar as these can be extracted from the texts of the scrolls. It is fully to be expected that some of these traits might tend to resemble one group (the Sadducees, for example) while others, possibly, another group (or groups).

THE CALENDAR

Identifying an ideological or spiritual movement is a tricky matter. (Think of "Romanticism" or "Post-modernism.") One may identify the movement by its leading ideas or dogmas, or sometimes by its characteristic linguistic expressions. It is not always easy to tell when leading ideas are distinctive marks of movements and when they are no more than independent reactions to prominent elements in the *Zeitgeist*. Many of the distinctive traits of the scrolls community have already been discussed above in the context of the attempt to establish the sectarian nature of this community. I want at this point to bring up the matter of the calendar. It is a striking feature of the Dead Sea group, about whose distinctiveness and centrality to that community there can be no doubt. Any attempt to identify the scrolls sect, or to provide an operational definition for it, must pay particular attention to the sectarians' calendar and to the implications of their adherence to it.

A Deviant Calendar

The sectarian calendar has been studied thoroughly and much is known about it. It plays a role, sometimes a major role, in many of the scrolls texts. In contrast to the regular Jewish calendar that is lunar, the sectarian calendar is solar. The year according to this calendar has 364 days, a neat number that divides by 4 (quarters) and 7 (weeks). This year is about a day and a quarter shorter than the natural solar year, so the calendar needs to be supplemented by some method of intercalation. However, we do not know anything about the method the scrolls sectarians used, nor indeed do we know whether they had such a method at all.

The calendar is divided into four quarters, each consisting of thirteen weeks and beginning always on a Wednesday (the day the sun and moon were created). It specifies the sect's holidays and festivals, both canonical and non-canonical.[14] Not only is the date of each holiday given, but also the fixed day of the week on which it falls (this is not possible with a lunar calendar), as well as the name of the priestly guard (*"mishmeret"*) associated with it. Much is known, too, about the sect's controversial method concerning when to begin counting the days of the *"Omer"* – that is, when to begin counting the forty-nine days following the Passover holiday and preceding the feast of Pentecost. This is one of the halakhic rules on whose interpretation the Dead Sea group is sharply divided from the Pharisees.

What is much less well known is how deviant this sectarian calendar actually was at the time. It is not altogether clear whether or not the calendar of the Dead Sea community broke with a well-established norm. Put differently, it is not altogether clear to what an extent the lunar calendar, which is the normative calendar governing Jewish life in the last two millennia, had already been unequivocally established as binding and authoritative before the fall of Jerusalem in 70 CE. It is possible that it was, but it is also consistent with the historical evidence that it was not.

The balance of scholarly opinions nowadays is that two parallel calendars might have coexisted in Judaea ever since the time of the Babylonian exile and the beginning of the Second Commonwealth era. One was the Babylonian lunar calendar, which functioned as the secular, administrative

---

14 Non-canonical holidays are those not specified in the Bible. For example, in addition to the biblical feasts for the first fruit of barley (Passover) and of wheat (Pentecost), the calendar of the scrolls community includes feasts for the first fruit of wine and of oil (Yadin, 1977–1983, I, pp. 119–122).

calendar. The other might have been based on ancient Egyptian traditions. This was a traditional priestly calendar which apparently governed the work in the Temple since the time of the kingdom of Solomon, and it was solar. It appears that at some unknown point of time, perhaps early in the Hasmonean period, the lunar calendar was introduced into the Temple. A fierce struggle ensued between the traditional priestly circles that favored the First–Temple solar calendar and the new priestly circles that favored the lunar calendar (Elior, 1995).[15]

The divergence between the two calendars meant significant gaps in the calculations of the first day of the months, of the days of the festivals, and of the schedule of worship in the Temple. The literary evidence from this period is replete with traces of bitter controversies relating to different calendar–based calculations. Much of this is speculative, however, and there is much that we do not know about the extent to which the lunar calendar was already firmly established in the last two centuries before the Common Era. The least that can be stated with confidence is the following: the wider the consensus over the lunar calendar in the period in question, the more dramatic the deviance of the solar-oriented Dead Sea sect from it, and the more pronounced its isolationist, sectarian character.

What Difference does a Different Calendar Make?

Let us take a moment to reflect on the impact that a different calendar might have on the sectarian character of a group choosing to live by it. For comparison, consider first the practice of endogamy, i.e., of marrying only within a specified group. It is common to take this as a practice that most severely divides people and marks a sect apart.[16] As a second instance

---

15 It should be noted that a solar calendar, not necessarily identical in all its details with the Qumran calendar, was also adopted by other dissident groups such as the Samaritans, and later the Karaites. Saul Lieberman and Shemaryahu Talmon noted that the adoption of a dissident calendar had served as a major instrument in the hands of social reformers in Judaism ever since the time of the First Temple down the generations to the medieval sectarian secessions (Elior, 1995, n.10).

16 A striking passage in the Mishnah in effect tells us that the main reason why the House of Shammai and the House of Hillel did not become two separate sects is because they continued to intermarry. "Notwithstanding that these forbid what the others permit, and these declare ineligible whom the others declare eligible, yet the [men of] the

consider different dietary norms or varying degrees of strictness in the observance of shared dietary norms. These may set groups of people apart if what they entail in practice is that members of one group cannot share a table with members of another. (In Israel today this often happens when a son or a daughter in a non-observant family chooses to "return to the faith" and the family cannot sit at the same table thereafter.) It may well be the case that, within the Jewish context, living by a calendar that differs from that of the rest of the community is an even more radical mark of division than the two instances just considered.

A common calendar, wrote Durkheim, "expresses the rhythm of collective activities" (1915, p. 11). In the Jewish context this truth has added poignancy. As historian Shemaryahu Talmon puts it, "No barrier appears to be more substantial and fraught with heavier consequences than differences in calendar calculation…. An alteration of any one of the dates that regulate the course of the year inevitably produces a breakup of communal life." Referring specifically to the Dead Sea sectarians, Talmon goes even further: "One may venture to say that the deviation from the calendar of the mainstream community was for the Covenanters…a sign and symbol of their thwarting the authority of the contemporary public Jewish leadership…. Their opponents rightly interpreted this act as a proclamation of civil revolt" (1989, pp. 148–149).

Moreover, the solar calendar, which is based on multi-year astronomical calculations, is fixed. The length of its month and the dates of the festivals are all fixed and calculable in advance. They do not depend, as is the case with the lunar calendar, on human observation of (and testimony about) the lunar cycle. Nor do they depend on frequent intercalation interventions. These facts may help explain the sacred character of the solar calendar. They also help explain that the split between the adherents of the two types of calendar is not merely of a practical and technical nature but has spiritual and theological dimensions. For the adherents of the solar calendar, the holy days of the festivals were from eternity preordained by God. They are

---

School of Shammai did not refrain from marrying women from [the families of] the School of Hillel, nor the [men of] the School of Hillel from marrying women from [the families of] the School of Shammai" (Trac. *Yebamoth*, 1.4, p. 219).

part of a divine plan that divides human history into set periods, and they have been endowed to mankind from the time of Creation. The holiness of these days, on this view, is of their very essence: it is unmediated by any human action, intervention, or convention. From this perspective one can appreciate the deep-level connection between the fixed and preordained nature of the sectarians' calendar and their doctrine of predestination (Elior, 1995).

A conception that attaches preordained holiness to the days of the festivals is a recipe for fanaticism. There can be no toleration toward those who err in determining the timing of the festivals, even if they properly recognize and observe the festivals themselves. Those who do not observe the Day of Atonement on the "right," heavenly preordained day, therefore, cannot be benignly treated or safely ignored, as people who simply choose to follow a different tradition. Nor yet can they be merely castigated as wrong or mistaken. They must be taken for sinners, for transgressors of the worst possible kind.

A prominent manifestation of this attitude is to be found in the *Habakkuk Commentary*, where there is a reference to an attack upon the Teacher of Righteousness by his enemies. This attack takes place on the day that to the Teacher and to his followers is the Day of Atonement (1Qp*Hab*. 11:4–8). Such a premeditated attack is meant to achieve much more than the tactical advantage derived from the circumstance that on his holy day the Teacher of Righteousness would not be prepared to fight. (Compare in this respect Sadat's decision to attack Israel on Yom Kippur, 1973.) It is meant to make an ultimate, momentous point about "we" and "they," about belonging to the fold and being excluded from it.

IDEOLOGY OR PRACTICE?

What is the nature of the separation of the scrolls community from the mainstream community? Is it essentially over matters of religious ideology or of religious practice? Have these people split from the rest of the community primarily because of doctrinal, theological differences or primarily because of halakhic, interpretative differences?

This is not an easy set of questions to answer, and the different answers to them reflect different scholarly interests, anxieties, and agendas. My aim here is to explore some of the answers, inasmuch and insofar as they may help throw light on the nature of the scholarly programs involved. I note that there are two perspectives from which the differences between the research programs may be appreciated. One is the perspective of time: it stands to reason that scholarly agendas change and shift with the passage of time, and also that they would reflect general changes in the *Zeitgeist*. The second is the perspective of the scholars' religious allegiances: Dead Sea Scrolls research is marked by differences between Jewish and Christian agendas.

Christian Agendas

For convenience of reference let us divide the half-century of Dead Sea Scrolls (or DSS) research into the First and the Second Periods, the cut-off point being somewhere in the 1970s. Roughly speaking, during the First Period much of the research into the Dead Sea scrolls was in Christian hands: Roman Catholic priests and Presbyterian or Methodist ministers. In 1948, less than a year after the first scrolls were discovered in Cave 1, the State of Israel was founded and Jerusalem became a city divided between Israel and the Kingdom of Jordan. Since then, a constantly growing number of scrolls fragments were discovered in caves in the Judaean Desert by Bedouin and by archaeologists. Most of the research of these fragments was conducted in the so-called scrollery of the Palestine Archeological Museum (or PAM, later to be renamed the Rockefeller Museum) in Jordanian-controlled East Jerusalem. Israeli scholars had no access to this material, nor indeed did even any non-Israeli Jew. It may be of interest to note that, formally, the Palestine Exploration Society, later renamed the Israel Exploration Society, was a member of the Board of Trustees of the Palestine Archaeological Museum, which was a private museum. After 1948, however, the political situation prevented the Israeli Society's representatives from attending the board meetings.

Following the discovery in 1952 of Cave 4, with its thousands of scrolls fragments (fondly referred to by some as the "mother of all jigsaw puzzles") an international editorial committee was formed under the auspices of PAM. This committee consisted of scholars appointed by each of the four national schools – British, American, German, and French – of biblical or archaeological research in Jerusalem that were also represented on the PAM board. No Israelis or non-Israeli Jews were represented on this committee. Still, important material was in Israeli hands: the original three scrolls from Cave 1 that were purchased by Sukenik in 1947–48, and the additional four scrolls that were brilliantly acquired in 1954 by Sukenik's son, Yadin, in New York. This material was promptly published and made accessible to the entire scholarly community.[17]

It is of course not difficult to understand how it came about that the excitement surrounding the discovery of the Dead Sea scrolls in those early years was focused on the origins of Christianity. It is also important to keep in mind that as soon as the issues of authenticity and rough dating of the scrolls were settled, one question overshadowed all others and dominated the scholarly as well as the popular agenda: whether or not the scrolls would prove to be the missing link between Second Temple Judaism on the one hand, and the New Testament on the other. In other words, the question was whether or not "the Qumran documents reveal an anticipation of Christianity in the sect of the Essenes."[18]

A certain tension with regard to this question could soon be discerned among the Christian scholars who studied the scrolls early in the First Period. It was between conservative, orthodox theologians on the one hand, and more liberal or "freethinking" ones, on the other (Satran,1992, pp. 154–155). For the former, the idea that a Judeo–Christian link could be established produced anxiety in that it seemingly threatened to detract from the originality of Jesus and from the divine ascription of the Gospels. The theologically conservative researchers, therefore, tended to emphasize the differences between the texts of the scrolls and the New Testament. The more liberally inclined theologians-researchers tended to be animated by the idea of finding the missing link, and their agenda accordingly

---

17 For accounts of the story of the discovery and purchase of the first seven scrolls see Yadin, 1992 and Wilson, 1969; see also n. 1 to the Introduction, above.

18 The phrase is John J. Dougherty's; it captures Edmund Wilson's adoption of André Dupont-Sommer's hypothesis: Wilson, 1969, pp. 131–132.

encouraged the discovery and emphasis of points and themes of similarity between these sets of texts.[19]

Regardless, however, of whether the Christian scholars were concerned with emphasizing the similarities between the scrolls and the New Testament or rather with explaining them away, the themes they pursued in those early decades of research had much to do with these points of similarity, and were predominantly theological in nature. Among the themes discussed at great length during that period was, for example, the notion of baptism. This, along with the related notions of cleansing and atonement, and the role that "the Holy Spirit" may have played in this regard, loom large in several of the Qumran texts. In a similar vein, much attention was paid to the "sacred repast" of the *Rule of the Community* (or *Manual of Discipline*). In particular, the role of the broken bread and of the cup of wine in this meal and their possible connections to the Last Supper were much dwelt upon. Additional major themes of research in the early years included the concepts of salvation, perdition, and the last judgment; the figure of the Son of God; the doctrine of the Two Ways and the doctrine of predestination; echoes of messianism and of the apocalypse, and more.

At the same time that putative textual connections between the scrolls and the New Testament were being scrutinized, much scholarly effort was also invested in an enterprise of a broader scope. Attempts were made to establish doctrinal connections between the Qumran texts, on the one hand, and ancient hermetic Christian traditions and literature, on the other. For example, points of resemblance were carefully traced between the *Rule of the Community* and a Greek work known as the *Didache* (or *Teaching of the*

---

19   Stendahl, himself a liberal theologian, points out that the unconscious attitude of modern man is to "prove that there is something new in Christianity, something never heard of before," and to see Jesus as "the inventor of Christianity, and the church [as] the guardian of his patent and his copyright." Hence, he says, "we are badly prepared to receive the good news from the Qumran Scrolls." In his own view, "it is hard to see how the authority of Christianity could depend on its 'originality,' i.e., on an issue which was irrelevant in the time when 'Christianity' emerged out of the matrix of Judaism, not as a system of thought but as a church, a community" (Stendahl, 1992, pp. 3, 6, 16) For material regarding alleged attempts by First-Period religiously motivated scrolls scholars to "distance Christianity from the scrolls" see Shanks, 1992b and also Fitzmyer, 1992, pp. 167–170.

Twelve Apostles), which begins with the words: "There are two ways...".
Resemblance was also noted between the *Rule* and the *Shepherd*, a second-century work attributed to Hermas.[20] (Note: the name Hermas is not related to the adjective "hermetic".)

The Spiritual Picture

The picture of the scrolls sect that emerges from this Christian scholarly literature is of a highly spiritual community whose split from mainstream Judaism was spiritually motivated. The sect, commonly and unquestionably identified in the early years with the Essenes, is portrayed as an ascetic brotherhood of purity. It is further portrayed as having embarked upon a theological journey that was to distance it from normative Judaism and, eventually, lead to Christianity.[21] Membership in its ranks, says Stendahl, "was given a theological [and] eschatological significance.... They formed the community of the New Covenant. Through initiation and obedience, they were the elect ones" (1992, p. 7).

Not wholly unrelated to this ethereal picture is the striking tendency in the First Period of DSS studies to romanticize the sectarians. This tendency is manifest in many of the writings of the period, but perhaps nowhere more than in Edmund Wilson's highly influential book, *The Scrolls from the Dead Sea* (first published in 1955). In this volume Wilson provides the following descriptions of the "subduing and dreadful" Dead Sea landscape:

> And across the lake..., to the place to which our jeep has now brought us, the Essenes once resorted to worship God and to save their souls...; to turn away from the Way of Darkness and follow the Way of Light. Their monastery, built crudely of gray blocks of stone,

---

20 The presumed connections go even farther: "The guess has been hazarded by Pere Audet that [Hermas'] father had been a Jew who belonged to the Dead Sea Sect, and that, after the descent of the Romans in A.D. 70 (when the monastery was probably destroyed), he brought the boy to Rome and sold him" (Wilson, 1969, p. 76).

21 In this context, first-century Josephus may be regarded as a precursor of the twentieth-century Christian scholars: mindful of his Hellenistic and Roman audiences, he too tended to emphasize and dramatize the theological, or "philosophical," differences between the Essenes and the other two major parties.

The sun rises over the mountains of Moab and the Dead Sea.
The protruding structure in the foreground is the tower of the Qumran compound

© The Israel Museum, Jerusalem / by Avraham Hai

still stands, as was noted by Pliny, some distance away from the shore. The cliff rises steep behind it, and one catches sight, here and there, of the dark cracks of natural caves such as the one in which the scrolls were found.... The palms that were noted by Pliny as the only companions of the Essenes must have disappeared centuries ago. The only forms of vertebrate life that we see as we drive in toward the monastery are a hawk and a crow contending for some small animal that the crow has caught but that the hawk has forced him to drop.... There are scorpions and vipers here. (1969, pp. 42, 44.)

Wilson artfully strews his descriptions with passages from Josephus about the Essenes, intertwining them with passages from the *Rule of the Community*. Thus he draws a compelling image of the way of life of a highly spiritual community, highlighting "the horror of the world from which they have withdrawn but which, morally, they have been able to stand up to" (ibid., p. 33).

Changed Circumstances, Different Picture

This picture by no means dominates the field today. Over the years there have been significant changes in the trends of Dead Sea Scrolls research. Powerful external circumstances led, in the Second Period, to a manifold increase in the ranks of DSS scholars and transformed their composition. Among these circumstances one should note, in the first place, the changed political situation after the war of June 1967. For example, the Rockefeller Museum came under Israeli jurisdiction.[22] Another major factor of change, much later, was the highly publicized and successful international campaign waged in the late 1980s to "liberate" the scrolls, i.e., to break the monopoly of the editorial board over access to the unpublished Qumran texts.

---

22 While the scrolls came technically under Israeli jurisdiction in June 1967, it is important to note that Israel, conscious of the pressure of world public opinion, was reluctant to interfere with either the structure or the mandate of the international editorial committee. It took a long time before the influence of Israeli authorities and scholars started to be felt in DSS research. For this reason I did not choose to see the Second Period as beginning in 1967.

As a result, the Dead Sea scrolls as a field of research had not only begun to attract many more scholars, but a new kind of scholars. Many of these were Jewish researchers who were well trained in halakhic studies and in the Mishnaic and Talmudic literature. Also attracted were scholars interested in the period of the Second Commonwealth from a large variety of aspects and from a specifically Jewish perspective. Important to remember in this context is the circumstance that during the Second Period of DSS research two major scrolls were published that are of a highly significant halakhic import, namely the *Temple Scroll* and the *MMT* (in 1977 and 1994, respectively).

These and other factors combined in the Second Period to produce an overall picture that was remarkably different from that of the First Period. An alternative tendency developed among the Jewish scholars and became entrenched. It was to relegate the story of the Dead Sea sect to the Internal Affairs Department, as it were: to see the scrolls sect as an internal, Priestly–Jewish story, quite dissociated from anything Christian. This tendency leads to a very different reading of the documents. It calls for combing and scrutinizing the texts of the scrolls primarily through the prism of Jewish *halakhah* and its history.[23]

Whatever else can be said of this development, one thing is clear: that it is decidedly unromantic. It may, to be sure, arouse excitement within a particular circle of scholars, but for the wider public this development is experienced as a disappointment. "Initially, there were great expectations that the writings of the sect would reveal its members to be the precursors of a spiritualistic, evolving, antinomian religion stressing vision and spirit, not the meticulous observations of religious commandments" (Sussmann, 1994, p. 184). According to Sussmann, it gradually became clear however that the zealous fight being waged by the sectarians against their enemies

---

23 It is a historical curiosity that research into the *halakhah* of the scrolls in effect predated the discovery of the scrolls near Qumran by almost fifty years. It started with the study by Schechter of the Cairo Genizah document, which only later came to be identified as the *Damascus Document* (see Chapter Two, p. 67). The paradox is that since the archaeological discovery of the scrolls and throughout the First Period of their research the halakhic study was neglected.

was for "the supremacy of the halakhah in all its minute details, according to their own interpretation" (ibid.).

This alternative scholarly orientation reflects an alternative view of the nature of the secession of the scrolls sect from mainstream Second-Commonwealth Judaism. According to this view the impetus behind the sect's splitting off from the rest of the community had to do with strictness of religious practice rather than with conflicting doctrinal beliefs. Thus, in his commentary to *MMT*, Sussmann talks about "the sect's own conception of its uniqueness, and of what distinguished it from the rest of the Jewish community." His formulation of its uniqueness is unequivocal: "What distinguished it and served as the backbone of its sectarian polemic was not religious doctrines, theology, or national or political issues, but halakhah." And he adds:

> When the leaders of the sects face off...they discuss halakhic details, and not theological issues. It was over the halakhah that they fought, and because of it that they split. It is clear that the dispute had theological import and was laden with ethical and religious significance, but the practical manifestation of this conflict was to be found in the observance of the halakhah (1994, pp. 191, 196–197).[24]

On this view, the self-identity of the members of the scrolls sect had entirely to do with their own stringent interpretations of specific halakhic laws and commandments, predominantly relating to matters of purity and defilement. It had little to do with an alternative theological or spiritual outlook. At the same time, however, one must do justice to the scrolls sect and remember its adherence to the theological tenet of predestination. On this non-halakhic issue of doctrine the sectarians certainly differed from all

24 Consider also Talmon's remark: "We must seek the reasons for the overt breach between the normative community and the adherents of the Teacher of Righteousness first and foremost in the sphere of action rather than in ideas, i.e. in facts that constituted a tangible barrier between the parties in daily life" (1989, p. 148.) He also discusses in this connection the Mishnaic category of *rebellious elder*, a category to which the Teacher of Righteousness was apparently relegated because of his deviation from the mainstream halakhic tradition.

other Jewish denominations and movements, not only their contemporary ones but later in history as well. [25]

Examples and Further Observations

It was just noted that the prevailing scholarly view nowadays regarding the nature of the split of the scrolls sect from the majority of the people is that it was essentially over issues of differing interpretations of halakhic laws and commandments. It is worthwhile to glimpse at some particular laws and commandments that are central to the dispute. They are likely to strike us today as esoteric, if not marginal and even trivial. This in itself is of course not atypical of sectarian acrimonious splits in general. Here then are a few examples.

1   The dispute over the date of the reaping of the *omer*, the sheaf of barley whose flour is offered in the Temple in partial fulfillment of the commandments concerned with the new harvest. The dispute regarding the *omer* is about the exact timing of its reaping, and it focuses on the interpretation of the biblical expression "the morrow after the Sabbath" (Lev. 23:11). The Pharisaic interpretation, which has become the accepted interpretation in normative Judaism, takes "Sabbath" to mean the day of Passover, that is, the 15th day in the month of Nisan. Hence the reaping of the *omer* is decreed to take place on 16th Nisan. The scrolls sectarians, however, interpret "Sabbath" literally. They would thus have the *omer* reaped on the day after the first Saturday that occurs after the end of the Passover festival. Given their calendar, on which the first and the last days of the feast of Passover always occur on Wednesdays, the first Sabbath thereafter falls on 25th Nisan. Thus, their counting of the days of the *omer* starts on Sunday, 26th Nisan. The significance of this counting is that it determines the date of the Feast of Weeks (Pentecost),

---

25   For more on this, and for further sources, see Broshi, 2001a. Schwartz points out an interesting tension within the text of the *Rule of the Community* (which is where the predestination doctrine is spelled out) between what he refers to as practical, "tribal," priestly, pre-Hellenistic trends, and universalistic, spiritual, Hellenistic trends (1992, p. 181).

which takes place forty-nine days, i.e., seven weeks, later. The different interpretations regarding the date of the reaping of the *omer*, therefore, lead to a ten-day discrepancy in the celebration of Pentecost.

2   The dispute over priestly ritual cleanliness (main source: *MMT*). Here the question is when, precisely, does the priest, who is to perform the ceremony of the slaughtering of the red heifer, become ritually clean. Is he to be considered ritually clean as soon as he has taken a ritual bath (and is therefore called *tevul yom*), or only in the evening, after the sun has set upon him (when he is called *meurav shemesh*)?

3   The dispute over the composition of the sin offering (main source: the *Temple Scroll*). It seems that the sect held that the sin offering in the Temple should include cereal and libation offerings. This is contrary to the mainstream rabbinic interpretation of the biblical law according to which cereal and libation offerings should accompany every blood sacrifice except in the case of sin offerings.

More examples could be cited. Common to all of them is that they are all on the side of strictness.[26] These particular examples were chosen because they hold rather special interest when considered in light of the fact that the disputes they involve are largely devoid of any practical significance and application in the life of a group that has entirely separated itself from the Jerusalem Temple and from the service and worship associated with it. But this seems to have taken away none of the sectarian fervor that had led to the separation in the first place. This fervor continued to fuel the high-pitched eschatological expectations and the intense existence of the sect throughout its life of self-imposed exile in the total isolation of the desert. The Dead Sea sect broke away from the rest of the Second-Temple Commonwealth because of its unwillingness to compromise. The sectarians aspired to live up to a utopian ideal, a purist and severe ideal of relentless religious stringency.

---

26   Saul Lieberman refers to the sectarians as "ultra-pious extremists" (Sussmann, 1994, n. 29.) Further examples concern, e.g., the non-cleanliness of flowing liquids, the prohibition on the deaf to approach the purity of the Temple, the prohibition against bringing dogs to the entire area of Jerusalem, and more.

Some will surely insist that any split over degrees of strictness must have spiritual aspects. They might point out that focusing on minute matters of ritual practice masks from view an underlying theological significance and a deep moral and spiritual pathos. Or they might argue (perhaps along the line taken by Schwartz, 1992, p. 180) that even though the Qumran texts embrace a vision of the Torah as a system of strict practical commandments, the logic underlying these texts subversively contains the seeds of the complete opposite of this view: namely, that underlying the Qumran texts is the Paulinian logic of bold attacks aimed at undermining this vision of the Torah. Still, even those who tend to favor these arguments will not deny that the picture conveyed by the scholars of the First Period is considerably different from that of the Second Period regarding the nature of the scrolls sect and the animus behind its split from the rest of the people.

SCHOLARLY ANXIETIES AND MOTIVATED AGENDAS

I have already touched upon scholarly anxieties and agendas, whether explicit or hidden, in the context of discussing the predominantly Christian-dominated First Period of DSS research. I want now to point to some anxieties on the Jewish side too. These have to do, in part, with what was perceived as a threat to the authority of the masoretic (that is, traditional) text of the Bible. Others are related to the integrity of the corpus of Jewish law known as *halakhah*.

Recall, first, the apprehensions mentioned earlier in some conservative Christian circles about the possibility that the scrolls might prove to provide the missing link between the Old and the New Testaments. This was perceived as threatening insofar as the idea that Christianity organically evolved out of Judaism was taken to undermine the originality of Jesus. Parallel fears apparently existed among Jewish scholars too. In the first decade of scrolls research, eminent historian Y. F. Baer, for example, concerned with defending the integrity of normative Judaism during the Second Commonwealth period, considerably post-dated the scrolls. For him the entire corpus of the scrolls belonged not to any Jewish sect but to the early Christians. Other scholars in that first decade pursued various options designed to distance the scrolls from any possible Christian connection.[27]

Jewish tradition regards the entire corpus of the biblical texts as having been given to Moses on Mount Sinai. Not an iota has, or ever can be, changed in this text. And in fact until the 1950's most non-Jewish Western scholars who dealt with the problems of textual criticism of the Bible also regarded the masoretic text with extreme reverence that bordered on what Frank M. Cross refers to as "Masoretic Fundamentalism". Passages in the Greek Bible, the *Septuagint*, which differed from the received version, were believed to be "due to mistranslation, ignorance, bias, or willful correction" (Cross, 2000, p. 935).

However, with the discovery of the Dead Sea scrolls the scholarly outlook underwent a sea change. Evidence appeared for the first time to establish that the Greek translators of the Septuagint were far more faithful to the underlying Hebrew text than had been previously supposed. Except that the Hebrew text they had before them was now conjectured to have been a different one from the received, masoretic Hebrew text.

Let me spell this out in some detail. Of the almost nine hundred different texts found in the Dead Sea caves, roughly two hundred are biblical. Every book of the Bible (with the exception of the small book of Esther) is represented in the scrolls material, many of them in multiple copies. These documents predate the earliest Hebrew biblical texts that were previously known by about one thousand years. When texts of the biblical scrolls began to be compared with the masoretic text, the resemblance was striking. But precisely because the overlap was so nearly total, special attention was justifiably given to the rather rare inconsistencies. It then transpired that some of the differences between the scrolls' biblical texts and the masoretic text strongly correlated with the differences that had long been known to exist between the masoretic text and its Septuagint translation into Greek. It was thus reasonably inferred that earlier, pre-canonical *Ur*-versions of the Hebrew Bible were extant in the centuries immediately preceding the

---

27   Zeitlin's early attempt to prove that the scrolls were forged, Rabin's attribution of the scrolls to the Pharisees, and Roth's attribution of them to the Zealots may all be seen as springing from these scholars' concern to "Judaize" the scrolls (Daniel Schwartz, personal communication).

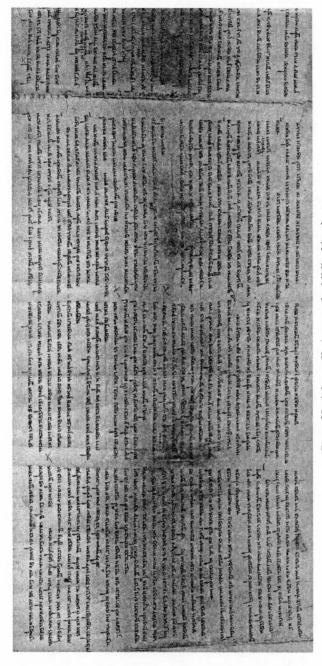

Part of Isaiah scroll. Among the biblical books,
it is the only one found in its entirety. (This copy is dated ca. 100BCE.)

© The Israel Museum, Jerusalem / by Avraham Hai

beginning of the Christian era. Some of these texts were presumably the ones copied by the scribes of the Dead Sea scrolls, and some of these same texts lay before the translators of the Septuagint. This theory naturally shook the scholarly field of textual criticism of the Bible and necessitated its cardinal revision.[28]

Additional anxieties concern the *halakhah* and come from Orthodox Jewish quarters.[29] These reflect a trend which – to echo the phrase "Masoretic Fundamentalism" invoked above – may perhaps be referred to as halakhic fundamentalism. They have to do with the extreme reluctance on the part of some Orthodox Jewish scholars to concede any process of internal development and evolution in the body of Jewish law known as *halakhah*. For orthodox believers the *halakhah* was revealed and passed on in the exact rabbinic form in which we know it today. This doctrine as well as the notion of the unity (or monolithic nature) of *halakhah* are unshakable tenets in normative Judaism. Hence the nervousness that may be felt in certain quarters by any text that appears to contain traces of a period in the life of the People of Israel in which the *halakhah* was still in flux.

For the scholars who share this nervousness, it largely frames their research agenda. These scholars are less concerned than their non-Orthodox Jewish colleagues about the question whether, on balance, the heterodox interpretations of biblical law that are expressed in such scrolls as the *Temple Scroll* and *MMT* (among others) are closer to the Pharisaic or to the Sadducean interpretations. Their own paramount concern is with the question whether or not the heterodoxy of the scrolls sect existed against the background of an existing normative orthodoxy, and whether or not the authority of this orthodoxy was commonly accepted regarding the relevant rulings and interpretations. It seems fair to say that some of

---

28 This paragraph glosses over many details and nuances. For more, see Tov, 1992.

29 In talking about the attitude of Orthodox Jews to the Dead Sea scrolls, it has to be clear that one is talking about academic scholars who are Orthodox Jews. Outside of academe, in the world of rabbinic, normative, Orthodox Judaism (i.e., in the world of the *yeshivot*) the scrolls are ignored. (An esoteric scholarly study that connects the ultra-Orthodox world in Jerusalem and the Dead Sea scrolls is Liebes, 1982.)

these scholars devote their scholarship to the attempt to show that this was indeed the case. Namely, to establish that a Jewish orthodoxy existed in the centuries that preceded the destruction of the Second Temple, and that this orthodoxy is substantially identical with the rabbinic orthodoxy of the last two millennia.

In this chapter I dealt with underlying conceptual issues. Underlying the question which sect authored the Dead Sea scrolls is the presupposition that it was a sect. In the course of justifying this presupposition, the notion of a sect had first to be examined, within a history–sensitive framework, both in religious and in non-religious, political contexts. In light of this examination the sectarian nature of the Dead Sea community itself had to be further probed and better understood. Prominent among the issues that were brought to bear in the discussion that ensued was the relationship between heterodoxy and orthodoxy. To the extent that sects express heterodoxy, I focused on the question whether by claiming that a group is a sect – and especially a religious sect – one is thereby committed to the existence of a background orthodoxy, against which the group protests and from which it deviates. And if so, what can scholars tell us about the existence and nature of the orthodoxy from which the Dead Sea sect was dissenting?

The questions relating to the nature of the orthodoxy that might, or might not, have reigned during the couple of centuries spanning the beginning of the Christian Era led me to consider the possible orthodoxy of the DSS researchers themselves and to ponder its implications. A further set of underlying issues was thereby brought up, one that touches upon yet another intriguing aspect of Dead Sea Scrolls research: the extent to which this research is ideologically motivated and directed. We saw how deep-rooted anxieties and wishes of scholars may have influenced the agenda of their research of the scrolls. But a word of caution is in order here. There is a thin but all-important line that divides research whose questions are shaped, in part, by the scholar's *Weltanschauung*, from research whose findings and conclusions are predetermined by the scholar's *Weltanschauung*. The former is scientifically legitimate while the latter is not.

This point was already made earlier, in connection with the question to what extent de Vaux's excavation of the site of Qumran could be described as wishful archaeology. It was in that connection, too, that the distinction was introduced and elaborated upon between the context of formation (discovery) and the context of confirmation (justification). This distinction bears revisiting here. One may point, for example, to the fact that Christian scholars focused on the sect's strict purity customs in their eagerness to explore the possible connections between these customs and Christian baptism. Or one may point to comments about the same issue made by Jewish scholars, anxious to establish the relationship of these purity customs to the normative halakhic requirements relating to ritual bathing or to the use of stone rather than clay vessels. To point out these agenda items is not thereby to discredit either set of comments. The fact that the emotional or ideological stakes that scholars might have in the subject matter of their research are high may account for the heat and excitement their inquiry engenders. At the same time it need not (even though it might) dim the light gained by the inquiry, nor need it taint its outcome. The line here is fine, and perhaps it cannot quite be drawn in principle and in the abstract. The arbiter of these issues is ultimately to be found in the fullness of the details.

Bibliography

Allegro, John M. (1960), *The Treasure of the Copper Scroll* (Garden City, NY: Doubleday and Co.).

Baigent, Michael and Richard Leigh (1991), *The Dead Sea Scrolls Deception* (London: Jonathan Cape).

Bar-Adon, Pesach (1977), "Another Settlement of the Judaean Desert Sect at Ein el-Ghuweir on the Shores of the Dead Sea," *Bulletin of the American Schools of Oriental Research* 227, pp. 1–25.

Baumgarten, Joseph M. (1997), "The Religious Law of the Qumran Community," *Qadmoniot* 114, pp. 97–100 (Hebrew).

Ben-Shakhar, Gershon, Maya Bar-Hillel, Yoram Bilu, and Gaby Schefler (1998), "Seek and Ye Shall Find: Test Results Are What You Hypothesize They Are," *Journal of Behavioral Decision Making* 11, pp. 235–249.

Ben-Yehuda, Nachman (2002), *Sacrificing Truth: Archaeology and the Myth of Masada* (Amherst: Humanity Books).

Broshi, Magen (2001a), "The Archaeology of Qumran: A Reconsideration," in *Bread, Wine, Walls and Scrolls* (London: Sheffield Academic Press, pp. 198–210; first published in Hebrew in Broshi et al. [1992], pp. 49–62).

———. (2001b), "Predestination in the Bible and the Dead Sea Scrolls," in *Bread, Wine, Walls and Scrolls* (London: Sheffield Academic Press), pp. 238–251.

———. (2003), "A Monastery or a Manor House? A Reply to Yizhar Hirschfeld," *Cathedra* 109, pp. 63–68 (Hebrew).

———. (2004a), "Response to Y. Hirschfeld, Review of J. Magness, *The Archaeology of Qumran*, JRA 16 (2003) 648–52," *Journal of Roman Archaeology* 17, pp. 761–763.

———. (2004b), "Qumran and the Essenes: Six Categories of Purity and Impurity," in Moshe Bar-Asher and Deborah Dimant (eds.), *Meghillot,*

Studies in the Dead Sea Scrolls, vol. 2 (Jerusalem: The Bialik Institute), pp. 9–20 (Hebrew).

Broshi, Magen and Hanan Eshel (2001), "Radiocarbon Dating and the Messiah before Jesus," *Revue de Qumran* 78, pp. 311–317.

———. (2004), "Qumran and the Dead Sea Scrolls: The Contention of Twelve Theories," in Douglas R. Edwards (ed.), *Religion and Society in Roman Palestine: Old Questions, New Approaches* (London and New York: Routledge), pp. 283–297.

Broshi, Magen, Sarah Japhet, Daniel Schwartz, and Shemaryahu Talmon, eds. (1992), *The Scrolls of the Judaean Desert: Forty Years of Research: Proceedings of the Jerusalem Symposium Commemorating Forty Years of Qumran Research, June 23–24, 1987* (Jerusalem: The Bialik Institute and The Israel Exploration Society; Hebrew).

Cansdale, Lena (1997), *Qumran and the Essenes: A Re-Evaluation of the Evidence* (Tübingen: J. C. B. Mohr).

Carnap, Rudolf (1962), *Logical Foundations of Probability*, 2nd ed. (London: Routledge & Kegan Paul).

Clarcke, David L. (1968), *Analytical Archaeology* (London: Methuen).

Cross, Frank Moore (1992), "The Historical Context of the Scrolls," in Shanks (1992), pp. 20–32. (An earlier version of this article was published in 1971 under a different title.)

———. (2000), "Reminiscences of the Early Days in the Discovery and Study of the Dead Sea Scrolls," in Schiffman et al. (2000), pp. 932–943.

Cross F. M. and Esther Eshel (1997a), "Ostraca from Khirbet Qumran", in *Israel Exploration Journal* 47, pp. 17-28.

———. (1997b), "The 'Yahad' (Community) Ostracon", in A. Roitman (ed.), *A Day at Qumran – the Dead Sea Sect and its Scrolls*, Israel Museum Catalogue no. 394, Jerusalem, pp. 38-40.

Crown, Alan D. and Lena Cansdale (1994), "Qumran, Was It an Essene Settlement?" *Biblical Archaeology Review* 20, pp. 24–35.

De Vaux, Roland (1973), *Archaeology and the Dead Sea Scrolls* (Oxford: Oxford University Press).

Donceel, Robert, et al. (1999–2000), "Antique Glass from Khirbet Qumran," *Institut Royal du Patrimoine Artistique, Bulletin* 28 (Bruxelles), pp. 9–40.

Donceel, Robert and Pauline Donceel-Voûte (1994), "The Archaeology of Khirbet Qumran," in Wise et al. (1994), pp. 1–32.

Donceel-Voûte, Pauline (1994), "Les ruines de Qumran reinterpretées," *Archeologia* 298, pp. 24–35.

Douglas, Mary (2001), *In the Wilderness: The Doctrine of Defilement in the Book of Numbers* (Oxford: Oxford University Press).

Durkheim, Emile (1915), *The Elementary Forms of Religious Life*, trans. S. W. Swain (London: Allen and Unwin).

Elior, Rachel (1995), "The Jewish Calendar and Mystical Time," in Uriel Simon and Rachel Elior (eds.), *The Hebrew Calendar* (Jerusalem: The Presidential Study Group on the Bible and Sources of Judaism), pp. 22–41 (Hebrew).

Elkin-Koren, Niva (2001), "Of Scientific Claims and Proprietary Rights: Lessons from the Dead Sea Scrolls Case", *Houston Law Review* 38, pp. 445-462.

Eshel, Hanan (1997), "The History of the Qumran Community and Historical Details in the Dead Sea Scrolls," *Qadmoniot* 114, pp. 86–93 (Hebrew).

———. (2003), "Qumran and the Scrolls – Response to the Article by Yizhar Hirschfeld," *Cathedra* 109, pp. 51–62 (Hebrew).

Eshel, Hanan, Magen Broshi, Richard Freund and Brian Schultz (2002), "New Data on the Cemetery East of Khirbet Qumran," *Dead Sea Discoveries* 9, pp. 135–165.

Eshel, Hanan and Zeev Safrai (2002), "The Copper Scroll: A Sectarian Composition Documenting Where the Treasures of the First Temple Were Hidden," *Cathedra* 103, pp. 7–20 (Hebrew).

Fitzmyer, Joseph A. (1992), *Responses to 101 Questions on the Dead Sea Scrolls* (New York: Paulist Press).

Flavius, Josephus (1927), *The Jewish War* (*Bellum Judaicum*), ed. and trans. H. St. John Thackeray (London: Loeb Classical Library), vol. 2.

Flusser, David (1997), "The Sect of the Essenes and Its Beliefs," *Qadmoniot* 114, pp. 94–96 (Hebrew).

Frank, Harry Thomas, "Discovering the Scrolls," in Shanks (1992), pp. 3–19.

Garcia Martinez, Florentino (1996), *The Dead Sea Scrolls Translated*, 2nd ed. (Leiden, New York, and Cologne: E. J. Brill).

———. (2003), "Greek Loanwords in the Copper Scroll," in F. Garcia Martinez and G. P. Luttikhuizen (eds.), *Jerusalem, Alexandria, Rome* (Leiden and Boston: Brill), pp. 119–145.

Ginzberg, Louis (1976), *An Unknown Jewish Sect* (New York: The Jewish Publication Society).

Golb, Norman (1995), *Who Wrote the Dead Sea Scrolls* (New York: Scribner).

Hacking, Ian (1965), *Logic of Statistical Inference* (Cambridge: Cambridge University Press).

Haran, Menachem (1993), "Archives, Libraries, and the Order of the Biblical Books," *The Journal of the Near Eastern Society* 22, pp. 51–61.

Harman, Gilbert (1965), "The Inference to the Best Explanation," *Philosophical Review* 74, pp. 88–95.

Hirschfeld, Yizhar (1998), "Early Roman Manor Houses in Judea and the Site of Khirbet Qumran," *Journal of Near Eastern Studies* 57, pp. 161–189.

———. (2003a), "Qumran: Back to the Beginning," *Journal of Roman Archaeology* 16, pp. 648–652.

———. (2003b), "Qumran during the Second Temple Period: Re-Evaluating the Archaeological Evidence," *Cathedra* 109, pp. 5–50 (Hebrew).

———. (2004), *Qumran in Context: Reassessing the Archaeological Evidence* (Peabody, MA: Hendrickson).

Howson, Colin and Peter Urbach (1989), *Scientific Reasoning: The Bayesian Approach* (LaSalle, IL: Open Court).

Humbert, Jean-Baptiste (1994), "L'espace sacré à Qumrân: Propositions pour l'archéologie," *Revue Biblique* 101, pp. 160–214.

———. (2003a), "Reconsideration of the Archaeological Interpretation," in Humbert and Gunneweg, 2003, pp. 419–425.

———. (2003b), "The Chronology during the First Century B.C.," in Humbert and Gunneweg, 2003, pp. 425–445.

Humbert, Jean-Baptiste and A Chambon, eds. (2003), *The Excavations of Khirbet Qumran and 'Ain Feshkha: Synthesis of Roland de Vaux's*

Field Notes (Fribourg: Academic Press; Goettingen: Vanderhoeck & Ruprecht).

Humbert, Jean-Baptiste and Jan Gunneweg, eds. (2003), *Khirbet Qumran et 'Ain Feshkha*, vol. 2 (Fribourg: Academic Press; Goettingen: Vanderhoeck & Ruprecht).

Jeffrey, Richard C. (1983), *The Logic of Decision* (Chicago: The University of Chicago Press; first published in 1965).

Kapera, Zdzislaw Jan (2000), "Some Notes on the Statistical Elements in the Interpretation of the Qumran Cemetery," *The Qumran Chronicle 9*, pp. 139–151.

Klayman, Joshua (1995), "Varieties of Confirmations Bias," in J. Busemeyer, R. Hastie, and D. L. Medin (eds.), *Decision Making from a Cognitive Perspective* (New York: Academic Press), pp. 365–418.

Kneale, William (1963), *Probability and Induction* (Oxford: The Clarendon Press).

Kugler, Robert A. (2000), "Priests," in Schiffman and VanderKam (2000), pp. 688–693.

Kuhn, Thomas (1962), *The Structure of Scientific Revolutions* (Chicago: The University of Chicago Press).

Laperrousaz, Ernest-Marie (1976), *Qoumrân: L'établissement essénien des bord de la Mer Morte: Histoire et archéologie du site* (Paris: A. & J. Picard).

Lapp, Paul W. (1961), *Palestinian Ceramic Chronology 200 BC –AD 70* (New Haven: American Schools of Oriental Research).

Liebes, Yehuda (1982), "The Ultra-Orthodox Community and the Dead Sea Sect," *Jerusalem Studies in Jewish Thought* 4, pp. 137–152.

Magness, Jodi (2002), *The Archaeology of Qumran and the Dead Sea Scrolls* (Grand Rapids, MI: Wm. B. Eerdmans).

———. (2005), "Hirschfeld's *Qumran in Context*", *Review of Biblical Literature*. [http://www.bookreviews.org]

Main, Emanuelle (2000), "Sadducees," in Schiffman and VanderKam (2000), pp. 812–816.

Miller, George A. and Philip N. Johnson-Laird (1976), *Language and Perception* (Cambridge, MA: Harvard University Press).

Milik, Joseph T. (1959), *Ten Years of Discovery in the Wilderness of Judaea,* trans. John Strugnell (Naperville: Alec R. Allenson Inc.).

——. (1962), "Le rouleau de cuivre provenant de la grotte 3Q (3Q15)," in Maurice Baillet et al. (eds.), *Discoveries in the Judaean Desert*, III (Oxford: The Clarendon Press), pp. 200–302.

The Mishnah (1933), trans. Herbert Danby (Oxford: Oxford University Press).

Nimmer, David (2001), "Copyright in the Dead Sea Scrolls: Authorship and Originality", *Houston Law Review* 38, pp. 1-217.

Norton, Jonathan (2003), "Reassessment of Controversial Studies on the Cemetery," in Humbert and Gunneweg (2003), pp. 107–127.

O'Dea, Thomas (1968), "Sects and Cults," in David L. Sills (ed.), *International Encyclopaedia of the Social Sciences* (New York: The Macmillan Company and The Free Press), vol. 14, pp. 130–136.

Patrich, Joseph (1994), "Khirbet Qumran in Light of New Archaeological Explorations in the Qumran Caves," in Wise et al. (1994), pp. 72–95.

——. (1998), "Was There an Extra Mural Dwelling Quarter at Qumran?" *Qadmoniot* 115, pp. 66–67 (Hebrew).

——. (2000), "Did Extra-Mural Dwelling Quarters Exist at Qumran?" in Schiffman et al. (2000), pp. 720–727.

Patrich, Joseph and B. Arubas (1989), "A Juglet Containing Balsam Oil (?) from a Cave Near Qumran," *Israel Exploration Journal* 39, pp. 43–55.

Philo Judaeus (1989), *Every Good Man is Free (Quod omnis probur liber sit)* and *Hypothetica: Apology for the Jews*, in Geza Vermes and Martin D. Goodman (eds.), *The Essenes According to the Classical Sources* (Sheffield: Sheffield Academic Press), pp. 19–30.

Pliny the Elder (1942), *Natural History*, trans. H. Rackham (London: Loeb Classical Library) vol. 2.

Popper, Karl R. (1959), *The Logic of Scientific Discovery* (London: Hutchinson).

Qimron, Elisha and John Strugnell (1994), *Qumran Cave 4, V: Miqsat Ma'ase ha-Torah (Discoveries in the Judaean Desert*, X) (Oxford: The Clarendon Press).

Reich, Ronny (1990), "Jewish Purity Baths during the Second Commonwealth and the Time of the Talmud," Ph.D dissertation, The Hebrew University of Jerusalem, 1990 (Hebrew).

———. (1995), "A Note on the Function of Room 30 at Khirbet Qumran," *Journal of Jewish Studies* 46, pp. 157–60.

———. (1998), "*Miqwa'ot* (Ritual Baths) at Qumran," *Qadmoniot* 114, pp. 125–128 (Hebrew).

Reichenbach, Hans (1961), *Experience and Prediction* (Chicago: The University of Chicago Press; first published in 1938).

Rengstorf, Karl Heinrich (1963), *Hirbet Qumran and the Problem of the Library of the Dead Sea Caves* (Leiden: Brill).

Roth, Cecil (1964–1966), "Qumran and Masada: A Final Clarification Regarding the Dead Sea Sect," *Revue de Qumran* 5, pp. 81–87.

Satran, David (1992), "Qumran and Christian Origins," in Broshi et al. (1992), pp. 152–159 (Hebrew).

Schechter, Solomon (1910), *Fragments of a Zadokite Work* (Documents of Jewish Sectaries, 1) (Cambridge: Cambridge University Press).

Scheffler, Israel (1964), *The Anatomy of Inquiry* (London: Routledge & Kegan Paul).

Schiffman, Lawrence H. (1992), "The Sadducean Origins of the Dead Sea Scroll Sect," in Shanks (1992), pp. 36–49.

———. (1994), *Reclaiming the Dead Sea Scrolls* (Philadelphia: Jewish Publication Society).

Schiffman, Lawrence H., Emanuel Tov, and James C. VanderKam, eds. (2000), *The Dead Sea Scrolls Fifty Years after Their Discovery* (Jerusalem: Israel Exploration Society).

Schiffman, Lawrence H. and James C. VanderKam, eds. (2000), *Encyclopedia of the Dead Sea Scrolls* (Oxford and New York: Oxford University Press).

Schwartz, Daniel R. (1992), "Qumran between Priestliness and Christianity," in Broshi et al. (1992), pp. 176–182 (Hebrew).

Shanks, Hershel, ed. (1992), *Understanding the Dead Sea Scrolls* (New York: Random House).

Shanks, Hershel (1992a), "Intrigue and the Scroll," in Shanks (1992), pp. 116–125.

———. (1992b), "Is the Vatican Suppressing the Dead Sea Scrolls?" in Shanks (1992), pp. 275–290.

Shavit, Yaacov (1994), "The 'Qumran Library' in the Light of the Attitude towards Books and Libraries in the Second Temple Period," in Wise et al. (1994), pp. 299–318.

Steckoll, Solomon H. (1968), "Preliminary Excavation Report in the Qumran Cemetery," *Revue de Qumran* 6, pp. 323–336.

Stendahl, Krister (1992), "The Scrolls and the New Testament: An Introduction and a Perspective," in Krister Stendahl (ed.), *The Scrolls and the New Testament* (New York: Crossroad; pp. 1–17; first published in 1957).

Stern, Menachem (1974), *Greek and Roman Authors on Jews and Judaism*, vol. 1 (Jerusalem: The Israel Academy of Sciences and Humanities).

Sussmann, Yaacob (1994), "The History of the Halakhah and the Dead Sea Scrolls," in Qimron and Strugnell (1994), pp. 179–200. (First published in Hebrew in Broshi et al. (1992), pp. 99–127.)

Tabor, James D. (2005), "Qumran Without Texts, and Texts Without Qumran: The Quest for Archaeological Objectivity," in K. Galor, J.-B. Humbert, and J. Zangenberg (eds.), *The Site of the Dead Sea Scrolls: Archaeological Interpretations and Debates*. Proceedings of the Conference held at Brown University, November 17-19, 2002 (Leiden, New York, and Cologne: E. J. Brill; forthcoming).

Talmon, Shemaryahu (1989), *The World of Qumran from Within* (Jerusalem and Leiden: The Magnes Press and E. J. Brill).

Thiering, Barbara (1992), *Jesus and the Riddle of the Dead Sea Scrolls* (San Francisco: Harper).

Tov, Emanuel (1992), "The Biblical Scrolls from the Judaean Desert and their Contribution to Textual Criticism," in Broshi et al. (1992), pp. 63–98 (Hebrew).

Troeltsch, Ernst (1931), *The Social Teaching of the Christian Churches*, trans. Olive Wyon (London: George Allen and Unwin; first edition in 1912).

Ullmann-Margalit, Edna (1978), "Invisible-Hand Explanations," *Synthese* 39, pp. 263–291.

———. (1983), "On Presumption," *The Journal of Philosophy* 80, pp. 143–163.

Ullmann-Margalit, Edna and Avishai Margalit (1992), "Holding True and Holding as True," *Synthese* 92, pp. 167–187.

VanderKam, James C. (1992), "The People of the Dead Sea Scrolls: Essenes or Sadducees?" in Shanks (1992), pp. 50–62.

Vermes, Geza (1998), *The Complete Dead Sea Scrolls in English* (New York: Penguin USA).

Vogel, Jonathan (1998), "Inference to the Best Explanation," in Edward Craig (ed.), *Routledge Encyclopedia of Philosophy* (London and New York: Routledge), vol. 4, pp. 766–769.

Wilson, Brian R. (1967), *Patterns of Sectarianism* (London: Heinemann).

Wilson, Edmund (1969), *The Dead Sea Scrolls 1947–1969* (London: Collins Fontana Library; a revised and expanded version of *The Scrolls from the Dead Sea* [London: W. A. Allen, 1955]).

Wilson, John (1978), *Religion in American Society: The Effective Presence* (Englewood Cliffs: Prentice-Hall).

Wise, Michael O., Norman Golb, John Collins, and Dennis G. Pardee, eds. (1994), *Methods of Investigation of the Dead Sea Scrolls and the Khirbet Qumran Site* (New York: Annals of the New York Academy of Sciences).

Wolters, Al (1994), "History and the Copper Scroll," in Wise et al. (1994), pp. 285–298.

Yadin, Yigael (1977–1983), *The Temple Scroll*, I-III (Jerusalem: Israel Exploration Society and The Shrine of the Book).

———. (1985), *The Temple Scroll: The Hidden Law of the Dead Sea Sect* (New York: Random House).

———. (1992a), *The Message of the Scrolls* (New York: Crossroad, Christian Origins Library; first Hebrew edition in 1957).

———. (1992b), "The Temple Scroll – The Longest Dead Sea Scroll," in Shanks (1992), pp. 87–112.

Yardeni, Ada (1997), "A Draft of a Deed on an Ostracon from Khirbet Qumran", *Israel Exploration Journal* 47 (1997), pp. 233- 237.

Zangenberg, Jurgen (2000), "Bones of Contention: 'New' Bones from Qumran Help Settle Old Questions (and Raise New Ones) – Remarks on Two Recent Conferences," *Qumran Chronicle* 9, pp. 51–76.

Zias, Joseph E. (2000), "The Cemeteries of Qumran and Celibacy: Confusion Laid to Rest?" *Dead Sea Discoveries* 7, pp. 220–253.

Index

(Note: items and names appearing in footnotes only are not included in the index.)